Crochet Coats™

2

12

22

34

Swinging Single Coat

SKILL LEVEL

INTERMEDIATE

FINISHED SIZES

Instructions given fit size small; changes for medium, large, X-large, 2X-large and 3X-large are in [ ].

FINISHED GARMENT MEASUREMENTS

Bust: 38¾ inches *(small)* [42¾ inches *(medium)*, 46¾ inches *(large)*, 50¾ inches *(X-large)*, 54¾ inches *(2X-large)*, 58¾ inches *(3X-large)*]

MATERIALS

- Lion Brand Vanna's Choice medium (worsted) weight yarn (3½ oz/ 170 yds/ 100g per skein): 10 [11, 12, 13, 14, 15] skeins #158 golden yellow 
- Size J/10/6mm crochet hook or size needed to obtain gauge
- Tapestry needle
- Sewing needle
- Matching sewing thread
- ⅞-inch buttons: 6

GAUGE

Yoke and Collar: 10 pattern sts = 3 inches; 14 pattern rows = 4 inches
Body and Sleeves: 6 V-sts = 4 inches; 9 rows = 4 inches
Take time to check gauge.

PATTERN NOTES

Chain-2 at beginning of row or round counts as first half double crochet unless otherwise stated.

Join with slip stitch as indicated unless otherwise stated.

Yoke is crocheted first, from back to front with short rows, creating the shoulder slope.

Upper bodice and back are crocheted from the yoke to the bottom of armholes, and then joined.

Remainder of body is crocheted in one piece from armholes down.

Collar is crocheted directly into neckline.

When extended stitches are used, an extended single crochet is used in place of a slip stitch.

SPECIAL STITCHES

Extended single crochet (ext sc): Insert hook in st indicated, yo, pull lp through, yo, pull through 1 lp on hook (*first step*), yo, pull through 2 lps on hook.

Extended half double crochet (ext hdc): Yo, insert hook in st indicated, yo, pull lp through, yo, pull through 1 lp on hook (*first step*), yo, pull through 3 lps on hook.

V-stitch (V-st): (Ext sc, ch 1, ext sc) in place indicated.

INSTRUCTIONS
COAT
YOKE

Row 1: Beg at bottom edge of Back, ch 46 [50, 54, 54, 58, 58], sk first 2 chs, [sl st in next ch, hdc in next ch] across, turn. (*22 [24, 26, 26, 28, 28] sl sts, 22 [24, 26, 26, 28, 28] hdc*)

Row 2: (RS): Ch 2 (*see Pattern Notes*), [sl st in next hdc, hdc in next sl st] across, to last hdc, sl st in last hdc, leaving last sl st and ch-2 unworked, turn.

Row 3: Ch 2, [sl st in next hdc, hdc in next sl st] across, ending with sl st in last hdc, turn.

Next rows: Rep last row 9 [11, 11, 11, 13, 13] times.

LEFT SHOULDER

Row 1: Ch 2, [sl st in next hdc, hdc in next sl st] 6 [7, 7, 7, 8, 8] times, sl st in next hdc, leaving rem sts unworked, turn. (*7 [8, 8, 8, 9, 9] sl sts, 7 [8, 8, 8, 9, 9] hdc*)

Row 2 (short row): Ch 2, [sl st in next hdc, hdc in next sl st] 3 [3, 3, 3, 4, 4] times, sl st in next hdc, leaving rem sts unworked, turn. (*4 [4, 4, 4, 5, 5] sl sts, 4 [4, 4, 4, 5, 5] hdc*)

Row 3: Ch 2, [sl st in next hdc, hdc in next sl st] across, sl st in last hdc, turn.

Row 4: Ch 2, [sl st in next hdc, hdc in next sl st] across, sl st in last hdc, now working in sts 2 rows below, [hdc in next sl st, sl st in next hdc] across, turn. (*7 [8, 8, 8, 9, 9] sl sts, 7 [8, 8, 8, 9, 9] hdc*)

Row 5: Ch 2, [sl st in next hdc, hdc in next sl st] across, sl st in last hdc, turn.

Rows 6–9: Rep rows 2–5.

Next rows: [Rep row 5] 2 [2, 2, 4, 4, 4] times.

LEFT FRONT NECKLINE
Row 1: Ch 3, sk first 2 chs, sl st in next ch, hdc in first sl st, [sl st in next hdc, hdc in next sl st] across, sl st in last hdc, turn. *(8 [9, 9, 9, 10, 10] sl sts, 8 [9, 9, 9, 10, 10] hdc)*

Row 2: Ch 2, [sl st in next hdc, hdc in next sl st] across, sl st in last hdc, turn.

Next rows: [Rep rows 1 and 2 alternately] 1 [1, 1, 2, 2, 3] time(s). *(9 [10, 10, 11, 12, 13] sl sts, 9 [10, 10, 11, 12, 13] hdc at end of last row)*

Next row: Ch 7 [9, 9, 11, 13, 15], sk first 2 chs, [sl st in next ch, hdc in next ch] 2 [3, 3, 4, 5, 6] times, sl st in next ch, [hdc in next sl st, sl st in next hdc] across, turn. *(12 [14, 14, 16, 18, 20] sl sts, 12 [14, 14, 16, 18, 20] hdc)*

LEFT FRONT
Row 1: Ch 2, [sl st in next hdc, hdc in next sl st] across, sl st in last hdc, turn.

Next rows: Rep last row 4 [4, 6, 4, 4, 4] times.

LEFT UPPER BODICE
Row 1: Ch 1, [V-st *(see Special Stitches)* in next hdc, sk next sl st] across, ext sc *(see Special Stitches)* in last hdc, turn. *(11 [13, 13, 15, 17, 19] V-sts, 1 ext sc)*

Row 2: Ch 1, V-st in first ext sc, V-st in each ch-1 sp across, turn. *(12 [14, 14, 16, 18, 20] V-sts)*

Row 3: Ch 1, V-st in each ch-1 sp across, ext sc in last ext sc on last V-st, turn. *(12 [14, 14, 16, 18, 20] V-st, 1 ext sc)*

Next rows: [Rep rows 2 and 3 alternately] twice, turn. *(14 [16, 16, 18, 20, 22] V-sts, 1 ext sc at end of last row)*

LARGE, X-LARGE, 2X-LARGE & 3X-LARGE SIZES ONLY
Next row: Ch 1, ext sc in first ext sc, V-st in each ch-1 sp across, turn.

Next row: Ch 1, V-st in each ch-1 sp across, ext sc in last ext sc, turn.

X-LARGE, 2X-LARGE & 3X-LARGE SIZES ONLY
Next row: Ch 1, ext sc in first ext sc, V-st in each ch-1 sp across, turn.

Next row: Ch 1, V-st in each ch-1 sp across, ext sc in last ext sc, turn.

ALL SIZES
Fasten off.

BACK UPPER BODICE
Row 1: With RS facing, working in starting ch on opposite side of row 1 on Yoke, **join** *(see Pattern Notes)* in first ch, V-st in same ch, [sk next ch, V-st in next ch] across, turn. *(22 [24, 26, 26, 28, 28] V-sts)*

Row 2: Ch 1, ext sc in first ext sc, V-st in each ch-1 sp across, ext sc in last ext sc. *(22 [24, 26, 26, 28, 28] V-sts, 2 ext sc)*

Row 3: Rep row 2.

Row 4: Ch 1, V-st in first ext sc, V-st in each ch-1 sp across, V-st in last ext sc. *(24 [26, 28, 28, 30, 30] V-sts)*

Next rows: [Rep row 2] 2 [2, 2, 3, 3, 2] times. *(24 [26, 28, 28, 30, 30] V-sts, 2 ext sc at end of last row)*

Next row(s): [Rep row 4] 1 [1, 3, 4, 4, 5] time(s). Fasten off. *(26 [28, 34, 36, 38, 40] V-sts)*

RIGHT SHOULDER
Row 1: On WS of Back Yoke, sk next 16 [16, 20, 16, 18, 20] sts *(back neck edge)* from Left Shoulder, join in next st, ch 2, sl st in same st, [hdc in next sl st, sl st in next hdc] across, turn. *(7 [8, 8, 8, 9, 9] sl sts, 7 [8, 8, 8, 9, 9] hdc)*

Row 2: Ch 2, [sl st in next hdc, hdc in next sl st] across, sl st in last hdc, turn.

Row 3 (short row): Ch 2, [sl st in next hdc, hdc in next sl st] 3 [3, 4, 3, 4, 4] times, sl st in next hdc, leaving rem sts unworked, turn. *(4 [4, 4, 4, 5, 5] sl sts, 4 [4, 4, 4, 5, 5] hdc)*

Row 4: Ch 2, [sl st in next hdc, hdc in next sl st] across, sl st in last hdc, turn.

Row 5: Ch 2, [sl st in next hdc, hdc in next sl st] across, sl st in last hdc, now working in sts 2 rows below, [hdc in next sl st, sl st in next hdc] across, turn. *(7 [8, 8, 8, 9, 9] sl sts, 7 [8, 8, 8, 9, 9] hdc)*

Rows 6–9: Rep rows 2–5.

Next rows: [Rep row 2] 2 [2, 2, 4, 4, 4] times.

RIGHT FRONT NECKLINE

Row 1: Ch 2, [sl st in next hdc, hdc in next sl st] across, ext sc in last hdc, **ext hdc** *(see Special Stitches)* in first step of last ext sc, ext sc in first step of last ext hdc, turn. *(8 [9, 9, 9, 10, 10] sl sts, 8 [9, 9, 9, 10, 10] hdc)*

Row 2: Ch 2, [sl st in next hdc, hdc in next sl st] across, sl st in last hdc, turn.

Next rows: [Rep rows 1 and 2 alternately] 1 [1, 1, 2, 2, 3] time(s). *(9 [10, 10, 11, 12, 13] sl sts, 9 [10, 10, 11, 12, 13] hdc)*

Next row: Ch 2, [sl st in next hdc, hdc in next sl st] across, ext sc in last hdc, [ext hdc in first step of last ext sc, ext sc in first step of last ext hdc] 3 [4, 4, 5, 6, 7] times, turn. *(12 [14, 14, 16, 18, 20] sl sts, 12 [14, 14, 16, 18, 20] hdc)*

RIGHT FRONT & BUTTONHOLE
Row 1: Ch 2, [sl st in next hdc, hdc in next sl st] across, sl st in last hdc, turn.

Row 2: Ch 2, sl st in next hdc, hdc in next sl st, ch 2 *(buttonhole)*, sk next 2 sts, [sl st in next hdc, hdc in next sl st] across, turn. *(11 [13, 13, 15, 17, 19] sl sts, 11 [13, 13, 15, 17, 19] hdc)*

Row 3: Ch 2, sl st in next hdc, *hdc in next sl st, sl st in next hdc*, rep between * across to ch-2, hdc in next ch, sl st in next ch, rep between * once, turn. *(12 [14, 14, 16, 18, 20] sl sts, 12 [14, 14, 16, 18, 20] hdc)*

Next rows: [Rep row 1] 2 [2, 4, 2, 2, 2] times.

RIGHT UPPER BODICE
Row 1: Ch 1, ext sc in first hdc, [sk next sl st, V-st in next hdc] across, turn. *(11 [13, 13, 15, 17, 19] V-sts, 1 ext sc)*

Row 2: Ch 1, V-st in each ch-1 sp across, V-st in last ext sc, turn. *(12 [14, 14, 16, 18, 20] V-sts)*

Row 3: Ch 1, ext sc in first ext sc, V-st in each ch-1 sp across, turn. *(12 [14, 14, 16, 18, 20] V-sts, 1 ext sc)*

Next rows: [Rep rows 2 and 3] 1 [1, 2, 2, 2, 2] time(s). *(13 [15, 16, 18, 20, 22] V-sts, 1 ext sc at end of last row)*

RIGHT UPPER BODICE & BUTTONHOLE
SMALL & MEDIUM SIZES ONLY
Row 1: Ch 1, 2 ext sc in first ch-1 sp, ch 2 *(buttonhole)*, 2 ext sc in next ch-1 sp, V-st in each ch-1 sp across, V-st in last ext sc, turn. *(12 [14 V-sts], 6 ext sc)*

LARGE, X-LARGE, 2X-LARGE & 3X-LARGE SIZES ONLY
Row [1]: Ch 1, 2 ext sc in first ch-1 sp, ch 2 *(buttonhole)*, 2 ext sc in next ch-1 sp, V-st in each ch-1 sp across, ext sc in last ext sc, turn. *([14, 16, 18, 20] V-sts, 5 ext sc)*

ALL SIZES
Row 2: Ch 1, ext sc in first ext sc, V-st in each ch-1 sp across, sk next 2 ext sc, V-st in next ext sc, sk next ch-2, V-st in next ext sc, turn. *(14 [16, 16, 18, 20, 22] V-sts, 1 ext sc)*

X-LARGE, 2X-LARGE & 3X-LARGE SIZES ONLY
Row [3]: Ch 1, V-st in each ch-1 sp across, ext sc in last ext sc, turn.

Row [4]: Ch 1, ext sc in first ext sc, V-st in each ch-1 sp across, turn.

BODY
ALL SIZES
Row 1: Ch 1, V-st in each ch-1 sp across, V-st in last ext sc, ch 3, V-st in each ch-1 sp of Back, ch 3, V-st in first ext sc of Left Front, V-st in each ch-1 sp across, turn. *(56 [62, 68, 74, 80, 86] V-sts)*

Row 2: Ch 1, *V-st in ch-1 sp of each V-st** across to ch-3, sk next ch, V-st in next ch, sk next ch, rep from * across, ending last rep at **, turn. *(58 [64, 70, 76, 82, 88] V-st)*

Row 3: Ch 1, V-st in ch sp of each V-st across, turn.

Next rows: Rep last row 3 [3, 5, 3, 3, 3] times.

Next row: Ch 1, 2 ext sc in first ch-1 sp, ch 2 *(buttonhole)*, 2 ext sc in next ch-1 sp, ◊[V-st in ch sp of next V-st]◊ 12 [14, 15, 17, 18, 20] times, *(V-st, ch 1, ext sc) in next ch-1 sp*, rep between ◊ 28 [30, 34, 36, 40, 42] times, rep between * once, rep between ◊ 14 [16, 17, 19, 20, 22] times, turn. *(56 [62, 68, 74, 80, 86] V-sts, 6 ext sc)*

Next row: Ch 1, V-st in each ch-1 sp across, sk next 2 ext sc, V-st in next ext sc, sk next ch-2, V-st in next ext sc, turn. *(60 [66, 72, 78, 84, 90] V-sts)*

Next rows: [Rep row 3] 6 [6, 8, 8, 8, 8] times.

Next row: Ch 1, 2 ext sc in first ch-1 sp, ch 2 *(buttonhole)*, 2 ext sc in next ch-1 sp, ◊[V-st in next ch-1 sp]◊ 12 [14, 15, 17, 18, 20] times, *(V-st, ch 1, ext sc) in next ch-1 sp * once, rep between ◊ 30 [32, 36, 38, 42, 44] times, rep between * once, rep between ◊ 14 [16, 17, 19, 20, 22] times, turn. *(58 [64, 70, 76, 82, 88] V-sts, 6 ext sc)*

Next row: Ch 1, V-st in each ch-1 sp across, sk next 2 ext sc, V-st in next ext sc, sk next ch-2, V-st in next ext sc, turn. *(62 [68, 74, 80, 86, 92] V-sts)*

Next rows: [Rep row 3] 6 [6, 8, 8, 8, 8] times.

Next row: Ch 1, 2 ext sc in first ch-1 sp, ch 2 *(buttonhole)*, 2 ext sc in next ch-1 sp, ◊[V-st in ch-1 sp of next V-st]◊ 13 [15, 16, 18, 19, 21] times, *(V-st, ch 1, ext sc) in next ch-1 sp*, rep between ◊ 30 [32, 36, 38, 42, 44] times, rep between * once, rep between ◊ 15 [17, 18, 20, 21, 23] times, turn. *(60 [66, 72, 78, 84, 90] V-sts, 6 ext sc)*

Next row: Ch 1, V-st in each ch-1 sp across, sk next 2 ext sc, V-st in next ext sc, sk next ch-2, V-st in next ext sc, turn. *(64 [70, 76, 82, 88, 94] V-sts)*

Next rows: [Rep row 3] 6 [6, 8, 8, 8, 8] times.

Next row: Ch 1, 2 ext sc in first ch-1 sp, ch 2 *(buttonhole)*, 2 ext sc in next ch-1 sp, ◊[V-st in ch-1 sp of next V-st]◊ 13 [15, 16, 18, 19, 21] times, *(V-st, ch 1, ext sc) in next ch-1 sp*, rep between ◊ 32 [34, 38, 40, 44, 46] times, rep between * once, rep between ◊ 15 [17, 18, 20, 21, 23] times, turn. *(62 [68, 74, 80, 86, 92] V-sts, 6 ext sc)*

Next row: Ch 1, V-st in each ch-1 sp across, sk next 2 ext sc, V-st in next ext sc, sk next ch-2, V-st in next ext sc, turn. *(66 [72, 78, 84, 90, 96] V-sts)*

Next rows: [Rep row 3] 8 [8, 6, 6, 6, 6] times.

Next row: Ch 1, ◊[V-st in ch-1 sp of next V-st]◊ 16 [18, 19, 21, 22, 24] times, *(V-st, ch 1, ext sc) in next ch-1 sp*, rep between ◊ 32 [34, 38, 40, 44, 46] times, rep between * once, rep between ◊ 16 [18, 19, 21, 22, 24] times, turn. *(66 [72, 78, 84, 90, 96] V-sts, 2 ext sc)*

Next rows: [Rep row 3] 8 [8, 6, 6, 6, 6] times. *(68 [74, 80, 86, 92, 98] V-sts at end of last row)*

Next row: Ch 1, ◊[V-st in ch-1 sp of next V-st]◊ 16 [18, 19, 21, 22, 24] times, *(V-st, ch 1, ext sc) in next ch-1 sp*, rep between ◊ 34 [36, 40, 42,

46, 48] times, rep between * once, rep between ◊ 16 [18, 19, 21, 22, 24] times, turn. *(68 [74, 80, 86, 92, 98] V-sts, 2 ext sc)*

Next rows: [Rep row 3] 7 [7, 5, 7, 7, 7] times. At end of last row, fasten off. *(70 [76, 82, 88, 94, 100] V-sts at end of last row)*

COLLAR

Row 1: With WS of Left Front neckline facing, sk next 3 [3, 3, 5, 5, 5] sts, join in next st, ◊[hdc in next st, sl st in next hdc]◊ 1 [2, 2, 2, 3, 4] time(s), working in ends of rows, *[hdc in next row, sl st in next row] 7 [7, 7, 9, 9, 10] times*, rep between ◊ 8 [8, 10, 10, 10, 10] times, rep between * once, rep between ◊ 1 [2, 2, 2, 3, 4] time(s), turn. *(24 [26, 28, 32, 34, 38] sl sts, 24 [26, 28, 32, 34, 38] hdc)*

Row 2 (RS): Ch 2, [sl st in next hdc, hdc in next sl st] across, sl st in last hdc, leaving joining sl st unworked, turn.

Row 3 (short row): Ch 2, [sl st in next hdc, hdc in next sl st] 3 [4, 4, 5, 5, 6] times, sl st in next hdc, leaving rem sts unworked, turn. *(4 [5, 5, 6, 6, 7] sl sts, 4 [5, 5, 6, 6, 7] hdc)*

Row 4: Ch 2, [sl st in next hdc, hdc in next sl st] across, sl st in last hdc, turn.

Row 5: Ch 2, [sl st in next hdc, hdc in next sl st] across, sl st in last hdc, now working in sts 2 rows below, [hdc in next sl st, sl st in next hdc] across, turn. *(24 [26, 28, 32, 34, 38] sl sts, 24 [26, 28, 32, 34, 38] hdc)*

Rows 6–8: Rep rows 3–5.

Row 9: Ch 2, ◊[sl st in next hdc, hdc in next st]◊ 4 [4, 4, 5, 5, 6] times, *(sl st, hdc) in each of next 4 sts*, rep between ◊ 10 [12, 14, 16, 18, 20] times, rep between * once, rep between ◊ 5 [5, 5, 6, 6, 7] times, sl st in last hdc, turn. *(28 [30, 32, 36, 38, 42] sl sts, 28 [30, 32, 36, 38, 42] hdc)*

Row 10: Ch 2, [sl st in next hdc, hdc in next sl st] across, sl st in last hdc, turn.

Row 11: Ch 2, ◊[sl st in next hdc, hdc in next st] ◊ 8 [8, 8, 10, 10, 12] times, *(sl st, hdc) in each of next 6 sts*, rep between ◊ 6 [6, 8, 8, 10, 10]

times, rep between * once, rep between ◊ 7 [9, 9, 11, 11, 13] times, sl st in last hdc, turn. *(34 [36, 38, 42, 44, 48] sl sts, 34 [36, 38, 42, 44, 48] hdc)*

Row 12: Ch 2, [sl st in next hdc, hdc in next sl st] across, sl st in last hdc, turn.

Next rows: Rep last row 6 [6, 6, 8, 8, 8] times. At end of last row, fasten off.

SLEEVE
MAKE 2.
CAP
Row 1: Ch 14 [14, 14, 18, 22, 26], ext sc in 2nd ch from hook, [sk next ch, V-st in next ch] across, to last 2 chs, sk next ch, ext sc in last ch, turn. *(5 [5, 5, 7, 9, 11] V-sts, 2 ext sc)*

Row 2 (RS): Ch 1, V-st in first ext sc, V-st in each ch-1 sp across, V-st in last ext sc, turn. *(7 [7, 7, 9, 11, 13] V-sts)*

Row 3: Ch 1, ext sc in first ext sc, V-st in each ch-1 sp across, ext sc in last ext sc, turn. *(7 [7, 7, 9, 11, 13] V-sts, 2 ext sc)*

Next rows: [Rep rows 2 and 3] 3 [3, 4, 5, 5, 5] times. *(13 [13, 15, 19, 21, 23] V-sts, 2 ext sc at end of last row)*

Next rows: [Rep row 2] 3 times. *(19 [19, 21, 25, 27, 29] V-sts at end of last row)*

Next row: Rep row 3. *(19 [19, 21, 25, 27, 29] V-sts, 2 ext sc)*

UPPER SECTION

Row 1: Ch 1, ext sc in first ext sc, V-st in ch-1 sp of each V-st, ext sc in last ext sc, turn.

Next rows: Rep last row 5 [17, 17, 3, 5, 7] times.

LOWER SECTION

Row 1: Ch 1, sk first 2 ext sc, V-st in each ch-1 sp across, ext sc in last ext sc, turn. *(19 [19, 21, 25, 27, 29] V-sts, 1 ext sc)*

Row 2: Ch 1, sk first 2 ext sc, V-st in each ch-1 sp across, turn. *(19 [19, 21, 25, 27, 29] V-sts)*

Row 3: Ch 1, V-st in each ch-1 sp across, turn.

Rows 4 & 5: [Rep row 3] twice.

Row 6: Ch 1, ext sc in first ch-1 sp, V-st in each ch-1 sp across to last V-st, ext sc in last ch-1 sp, turn. *(17 [17, 19, 23, 25, 27] V-sts, 2 ext sc)*

Row 7: Ch 1, ext sc in first ext sc, V-st in each ch-1 sp across, ext sc in last ext sc, turn.

Next row(s): Rep last row 3 [3, 3, 1, 1, 1] time(s).

Next rows: [Rep Lower Section rows in sequence] 2 [1, 1, 3, 3, 3] time(s). *(13 [15, 17, 17, 19, 21] V-sts, 2 ext sc at end of last row)*

Next row: Ch 1, ext sc in first ext sc, V-st in each ch-1 sp across, ext sc in last ext sc. Fasten off.

ASSEMBLY

Sew Sleeve seams.

Easing to fit, sew Sleeves into armhole openings.

TRIM

Sc evenly around RS of outer edges on Sleeves and Coat, with 3 sc in each corner.

FINISHING

Sew buttons to Left Front opposite buttonholes on Right Front. ∎

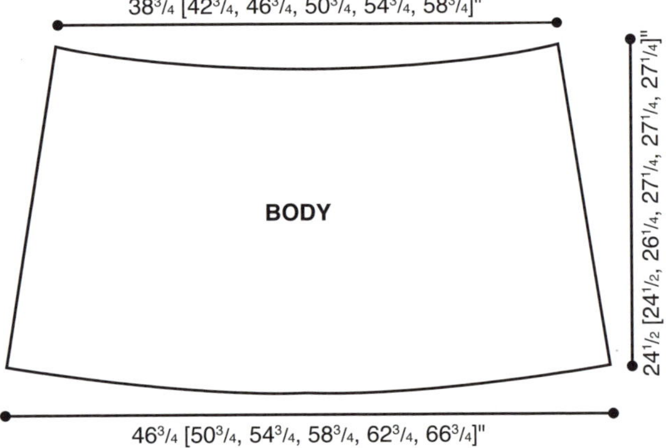

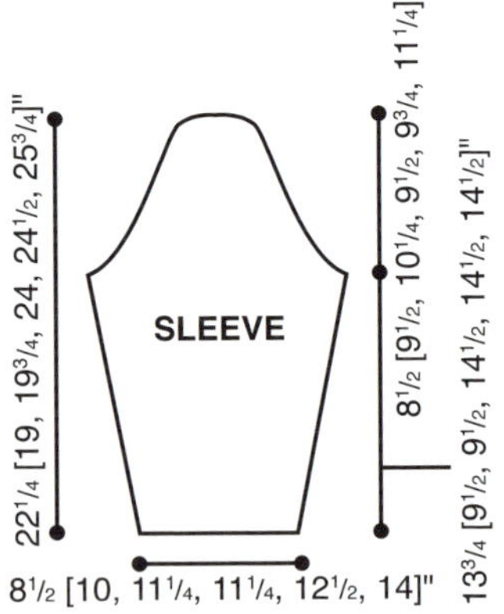

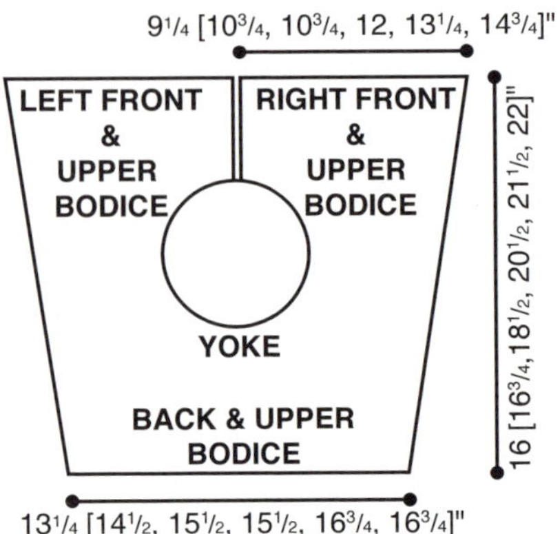

Textured Topper Coat

SKILL LEVEL

INTERMEDIATE

FINISHED SIZES

Instructions given fit size small; changes for medium, large, X-large, 2X-large and 3X-large are in [ ].

FINISHED GARMENT MEASUREMENTS

Bust: 37¼ inches (*small*) [40 inches (*medium*), 45¼ inches (*large*), 48 inches (*X-large*), 53¼ inches (*2X-large*), 56 inches (*3X-large*)]

MATERIALS

- Red Heart Super Saver medium (worsted) weight yarn (7 oz/ 364 yds/198g per skein): 5 [6, 6, 7, 7, 8] skeins #376 burgundy
- Size I/9/5.5mm crochet hook or size needed to obtain gauge
- Tapestry needle
- Sewing needle
- Matching sewing thread
- 1⅛-inch buttons: 3
- Stitch marker

GAUGE

16 sts = 4 inches; 12 rows = 4 inches
Ribbing: 4 sts = 4 inches; 5 rows = 2 inches
Take time to check gauge.

PATTERN NOTES

Join with slip stitch as indicated unless otherwise stated.

Chain-2 at beginning of row or round counts as first half double crochet unless otherwise stated.

Sleeve is worked in rounds, Body is then crocheted in one piece.

Collar is crocheted directly into neckline.

Begin and end each Pocket Welt with ends of 6–8 inches in length for sewing.

Begin and end each Pocket Sack with ends of 12–14 inches in length for sewing Sacks closed.

SPECIAL STITCH

Extended single crochet (ext sc): Insert hook in place indicated, yo, pull lp through, yo, pull through 1 lp on hook (*first step*), yo, pull through 2 lps on hook.

INSTRUCTIONS
COAT
RIGHT SLEEVE
CUFF

Rnd 1 (RS): Ch 28 [30, 32, 34, 36, 38], sl st in first ch to form ring, ch 1, [sc in next ch, dc in next ch] around, **join** (*see Pattern Notes*) in beg sc, **do not turn.** (14 [15, 16, 17, 18, 19] sc, 14 [15, 16, 17, 18, 19] dc)

Rnd 2: Ch 1, [sc in next sc, **fpdc** (*see Stitch Guide*) around next dc] around, join in beg sc. (14 [15, 16, 17, 18, 19] sc, 14 [15, 16, 17, 18, 19] fpdc)

Rnd 3: Ch 1, [sc in next sc, fpdc around next fpdc] around, join in beg sc.

Next rnds: Rep last rnd 2 [2, 2, 3, 3, 3] times.

Last rnd: Ch 1, [sc in next sc, fpdc around next fpdc] around, join in beg sc, **turn.**

SLEEVE

Rnd 1: Ch 2 (*see Pattern Notes*), *◊[sl st in next st, hdc in next st]◊ twice, (sl st, hdc) in next st, rep from * 4 times, rep between ◊ 1 [2, 3, 4, 5, 6] time(s), join in 2nd ch of beg ch-2, turn. (16 [17, 18, 19, 20, 21] sl sts, 17 [18, 19, 20, 21, 22] hdc)

Rnd 2: Ch 2, [sl st in next hdc, hdc in next sl st] around, join in 2nd ch of beg ch-2, turn.

Rnd 3: Ch 2, [sl st in next hdc, hdc in next sl st] around to last hdc rem, (sl st, hdc) in last hdc, (sl st, hdc) in last sl st, join in 2nd ch of beg ch-2, turn. (17 [19, 19, 20, 21, 22] sl sts, 18 [19, 20, 21, 22, 23] hdc)

Rnd 4: Rep rnd 3. (18 [19, 20, 21, 22, 23] sl sts, 19 [20, 21, 22, 23, 24] hdc)

Rnds 5–8: [Rep rnd 2] 4 times.

Rnds 9–10: [Rep rnd 3] twice. (20 [21, 22, 23, 24, 25] sl sts, 21 [22, 23, 24, 25, 26] hdc at end of last rnd)

Next rnds: [Rep rnds 5–10 consecutively] 3 [3, 3, 3, 2, 1] time(s). (26 [27, 28, 29, 28, 27] sl sts, 27 [28, 29, 30, 29, 28] hdc at end of last rnd)

UNDERARM SHAPING

Rnd 1: Ch 2, [sl st in next hdc, hdc in next sl st] around, join in 2nd ch of beg ch-2, turn.

Rnd 2: Rep rnd 1.

Rnd 3: Ch 2, [sl st in next hdc, hdc in next sl st] around to last hdc rem, (sl st, hdc) in last hdc, (sl st, hdc) in last sl st, join in 2nd ch of beg ch-2, turn. (27 [28, 29, 30, 31, 30] sl sts, 28 [29, 30, 31, 30, 29] hdc)

Rnd 4: Rep rnd 3. (28 [29, 30, 31, 32, 29] sl sts, 29 [30, 31, 32, 31, 30] hdc)

Next rnds: [Rep rnds 1–4 consecutively] 4 [4, 2, 0, 0, 1] time(s). (36 [37, 34, 33, 30, 31] sl sts, 37 [38, 35, 32, 31, 32] hdc)

Next rnds: [Rep rnd 3] 7 [10, 17, 24, 29, 32] times. (43 [47, 51, 55, 59, 63] sl sts, 44 [48, 52, 56, 60, 64] hdc)

Next rnd: [Rep rnd 1] 1 [0, 1, 0, 1, 0] time(s).

RIGHT SHOULDER

Row 1: Now working in rows, ch 78, sk first 2 chs (*first 2 chs count as first hdc*), *[sl st in next ch, hdc in next ch] across*, now working in last rnd of Sleeve, [sl st in next hdc, hdc in next sl st] around Sleeve, now working on opposite side of

starting ch (*ch 78*), rep between * once, sl st in last ch, turn. (120 [124, 128, 132, 136, 140] sl sts, 120 [124, 128, 132, 136, 140] hdc)

Row 2: Ch 2, [sl st in next hdc, hdc in next sl st] across, sl st in last hdc, turn.

Next rows: [Rep row 2] 2 [0, 2, 2, 0, 2] times.

A-LINE SHAPING

Row 1: Ch 2, [sl st in next hdc, hdc in next sl st] 27 [29, 31, 27, 29, 31] times, sl st in next hdc, turn. (28 [30, 32, 28, 30, 32] sl sts, 28 [30, 32, 28, 30, 32] hdc)

Row 2: Ch 2, [sl st in next hdc, hdc in next sl st] across, sl st in last hdc, turn.

Row 3: Ch 2, [sl st in next hdc, hdc in next sl st] across, sl st in last hdc, hdc in next sl st 3 rows below, [sl st in next hdc, hdc in next sl st] across, sl st in last hdc, turn. (120 [124, 128, 132, 136, 140] sl sts, 120 [124, 128, 132, 136, 140] hdc)

Rows 4–6: Rep rows 1–3.

Next rows: [Rep row 2] 2 [2, 4, 2, 6, 4] times.

Next rows: [Rep rows 1–6] 0 [1, 0, 1, 0, 1] time(s).

Next rows: [Rep row 2] 0 [2, 0, 2, 0, 4] times.

Next rows: [Rep rows 1–3 consecutively] twice.

POCKET OPENING

Row 1: Ch 2, [sl st in next hdc, hdc in next sl st] 91 [95, 99, 103, 107, 111] times, ch 19, sk next 19 sts, [hdc in next sl st, sl st in next hdc] across, turn. (111 [115, 119, 123, 127, 131] sl sts, 110 [114, 118, 122, 126, 130] hdc)

Row 2: Ch 2, [sl st in next hdc, hdc in next sl st] 18 times, sl st in next hdc, [hdc in next ch, sl st in next ch] 9 times, hdc in next ch, [sl st in next hdc, hdc in next sl st] across, sl st in last hdc, turn. (120 [124, 128, 132, 136, 140] sl sts, 120 [124, 128, 132, 136, 140] hdc)

RIGHT BODY

Row 1: Ch 2, [sl st in next hdc, hdc in next sl st] 27 [29, 31, 27, 29, 31] times, sl st in next hdc, leaving rem sts unworked, turn. *(28 [30, 32, 28, 30, 32] sl sts, 28 [30, 32, 28, 30, 32] hdc)*

Row 2: Ch 2, [sl st in next hdc, hdc in next sl st] across, sl st in last hdc, turn.

Row 3: Ch 2, [sl st in next hdc, hdc in next sl st] across, sl st in last hdc, hdc in next sl st 3 rows below, [sl st in next hdc, hdc in next sl st] across, sl st in last hdc, turn. *(120 [124, 128, 132, 136, 140] sl sts, 120 [124, 128, 132, 136, 140] hdc)*

Rows 4–6: Rep rows 1–3.

Next rows: [Rep row 2] 2 [2, 4, 2, 6, 4] times.

Next rows: Rep rows 1–6 once.

Next rows: [Rep row 2] 1 [1, 3, 3, 5, 3] time(s).

RIGHT FRONT

Row 1: Ch 2, [sl st in next hdc, hdc in next sl st] 57 [59, 61, 61, 63, 65] times, sl st in next hdc, leaving rem sts unworked, turn. *(58 [60, 62, 62, 64, 66] sl sts, 58 [60, 62, 62, 64, 66] hdc)*

Row 2: Ch 1, [sl st in next hdc, hdc in next sl st] across, sl st in last hdc, turn. *(58 [60, 62, 62, 64, 66] sl sts, 57 [59, 61, 61, 63, 65] hdc)*

Row 3: Ch 2, [sl st in next hdc, hdc in next sl st] across, sl st in last hdc, turn. *(57 [59, 61, 61, 63, 65] sl sts, 57 [59, 61, 61, 63, 65] hdc)*

Rows 4 & 5: Rep rows 2 and 3. *(56 [58, 60, 60, 62, 64] sl sts, 56 [58, 60, 60, 62, 64] hdc)*

Row 6: Ch 2, [sl st in next hdc, hdc in next sl st] across, sl st in last hdc, turn.

Next rows: [Rep row 6] 3 [3, 3, 5, 5, 5] times.

RIGHT BUTTON EXTENSION AND BUTTONHOLES

Row 1: Ch 2, ◊[sl st in next hdc, hdc in next sl st]◊ twice, *ch 2, sk next hdc and next sl st*, [rep between ◊ 8 times, rep between * once] twice, rep between ◊ across, sl st in last hdc, turn. *(52 [54, 56, 56, 58, 60] sl sts, 52 [54, 56, 56, 58, 60] hdc)*

Row 2: Ch 2, ◊[sl st in next hdc, hdc in next sl st]◊ across to ch-2 sp, *sl st in next ch, hdc in next ch*, [rep between ◊ 8 times, rep between * once] twice, rep between ◊ twice, sl st in last hdc, turn. *(56 [58, 60, 60, 62, 64] sl sts, 56 [58, 60, 60, 62, 64] hdc)*

Row 3: Ch 2, [sl st in next hdc, hdc in next sl st] across, sl st in last hdc. Fasten off.

LEFT FRONT AND BUTTON EXTENSION

Row 1 (RS): Ch 111 [117, 121, 121, 125, 129], sk first 2 chs *(first 2 chs count as first hdc)*, [sl st in next ch, hdc in next ch] across, sl st in last st, turn. *(56 [58, 60, 60, 62, 64] sl sts, 56 [58, 60, 60, 62, 64] hdc)*

Row 2: Ch 2, [sl st in next hdc, hdc in next sl st] across, sl st in last hdc, turn.

Next rows: [Rep row 2] 7 [7, 7, 9, 9, 9] times.

NECKLINE SHAPING

Row 1: Ch 3, sk first 2 chs, sl st in next ch, [hdc in next sl st, sl st in next hdc] across, turn. *(57 [59, 61, 61, 63, 65] sl sts, 57 [59, 61, 61, 63, 65] hdc)*

Row 2: Ch 2, [sl st in next hdc, hdc in next sl st] across, (sl st, hdc) in last hdc. Fasten off. *(57 [59, 61, 61, 63, 65] sl sts, 58 [60, 62, 62, 64, 66] hdc)*

BACK

Row 1: With RS facing, sk 7 [7, 7, 11, 11, 11] sts, join in next sl st, ch 1, [sl st in next hdc, hdc in next sl st] across, sl st in last hdc, turn. *(59 [61, 63, 65, 67, 69] sl sts, 58 [60, 62, 64, 66, 68] hdc)*

Row 2: Ch 2, [sl st in next hdc, hdc in next sl st] across, sl st in last hdc, turn. *(58 [60, 62, 64, 66, 68] sl sts, 58 [60, 62, 64, 66, 68] hdc)*

Next rows: Rep last row 14 [14, 14, 16, 16, 16] times.

Next row: Ch 3, sk first 2 chs, sl st in next ch, hdc in next sl st, [sl st in next hdc, hdc in next sl st] across, sl st in last hdc, turn. *(59 [61, 63, 65, 67, 69] sl sts, 59 [61, 63, 65, 67, 69] hdc)*

Next row: Ch 2, ◊[sl st in next hdc, hdc in next sl st] across◊, (sl st, hdc) in last hdc, ch 7 [7, 7, 11, 11, 11], sl st in first hdc of Left Front, rep between ◊, sl st in last hdc, turn. *(116 [120, 124, 126, 130, 134] sl sts, 117 [121, 125, 127, 131, 135] hdc)*

LEFT SHOULDER
Row 1: Ch 2, [sl st in next hdc, hdc in next sl st] across to ch, [sl st in next ch, hdc in next ch] 3 [3, 3, 5, 5, 5] times, sl st in next ch, [sl st in next hdc, hdc in next sl st] across, sl st in last hdc, turn. *(120 [124, 128, 132, 136, 140] sl sts, 120 [124, 128, 132, 136, 140] hdc)*

Row 2: Ch 2, *sl st in next hdc, hdc in next sl st, rep from * across, sl st in last hdc, turn.

Next rows: [Rep row 2] 0 [0, 2, 2, 4, 2] times.

A-LINE SHAPING
Row 1: Ch 2, [sl st in next hdc, hdc in next sl st] 27 [29, 31, 27, 29, 31] times, sl st in next hdc, leaving rem sts unworked, turn. *(28 [30, 32, 28, 30, 32] sl sts, 28 [30, 32, 28, 30, 32] hdc)*

Row 2: Ch 2, [sl st in next hdc, hdc in next sl st] across, sl st in last hdc, turn.

Row 3: Ch 2, [sl st in next hdc, hdc in next sl st] across, sl st in last hdc, hdc in next sl st 3 rows below, [sl st in next hdc, hdc in next sl st] across, sl st in last hdc, turn. *(120 [124, 128, 132, 136, 140] sl sts, 120 [124, 128, 132, 136, 140] hdc)*

Rows 4–6: Rep rows 1–3.

Next rows: [Rep row 2] 2 [2, 4, 2, 6, 4] times.

Next rows: [Rep rows 1–6] 0 [1, 0, 1, 0, 1] time(s).

Next rows: [Rep row 2] 0 [2, 0, 2, 0, 4] times.

Next rows: Rep rows 1–3 once.

Next rows: Rep rows 1 and 2 once.

POCKET OPENING

Row 1: Ch 2, [sl st in next hdc, hdc in next sl st] 91 [95, 99, 103, 107, 111] times, ch 19, sk next 19 sts, [hdc in next sl st, sl st in next hdc] across, turn. *(111 [115, 119, 123, 127, 131] sl sts, 110 [114, 118, 122, 126, 130] hdc)*

Row 2: Ch 2, [sl st in next hdc, hdc in next sl st] 18 times, sl st in next hdc, [hdc in next ch, sl st in next ch] 9 times, hdc in next ch, [sl st in next hdc, hdc in next sl st] across, sl st in last hdc, turn. *(120 [124, 128, 132, 136, 140] sl sts, 120 [124, 128, 132, 136, 140] hdc)*

LEFT BODY

Row 1: Ch 2, [sl st in next hdc, hdc in next sl st] across, sl st in last hdc, turn.

Row 2: Ch 2, [sl st in next hdc, hdc in next sl st] 27 [29, 31, 27, 29, 31] times, sl st in next hdc, leaving rem sts unworked, turn. *(28 [30, 32, 28, 30, 32] sl sts, 28 [30, 32, 28, 30, 32] hdc)*

Row 3: Ch 2, [sl st in next hdc, hdc in next sl st] across, sl st in last hdc, turn.

Row 4: Ch 2, [sl st in next hdc, hdc in next sl st] across, sl st in last hdc, hdc in next sl st 3 rows below, [sl st in next hdc, hdc in next sl st] across, sl st in last hdc, turn. *(120 [124, 128, 132, 136, 140] sl sts, 120 [124, 128, 132, 136, 140] hdc)*

Rows 5–7: Rep rows 2–4.

Next rows: [Rep row 3] 2 [2, 4, 2, 6, 4] times.

Next rows: Rep rows 2–7 once.

Next rows: [Rep row 3] 3 [2, 3, 2, 1, 4] time(s).

Next rows: [Rep rows 2–7] 0 [1, 0, 1, 0, 1] time(s).

Next rows: [Rep row 3] 0 [1, 0, 3, 0, 3] time(s). At end of last row, fasten off.

LEFT SLEEVE

Rnd 1: Now working in rnds, with WS of Left Back facing, sk 76 sts, join in next sl st, ch 2, [sl st in next hdc, hdc in next sl st] 43 [47, 51, 55, 59, 63] times, leaving rem sts unworked, join in

2nd ch of beg ch-2, **turn**. *(43 [47, 51, 55, 59, 63] sl sts, 44 [48, 52, 56, 60, 64] hdc)*

SMALL, LARGE & 2X-LARGE SIZES ONLY

Rnd 2: Ch 2, [sl st in next hdc, hdc in next sl st] around, sl st in last hdc, join in 2nd ch of beg ch-2, turn.

UNDERARM SHAPING

Rnd 1: Ch 1, **sl st dec** *(see Stitch Guide)* in next hdc and next sl st, [sl st in next hdc, hdc in next sl st] around, join in sl st dec, turn. *(42 [46, 50, 54, 58, 62] sl sts, 43 [47, 51, 55, 59, 63] hdc)*

Next rnds: [Rep rnd 1] 8 [11, 18, 25, 30, 33] times. *(34 [35, 32, 29, 28, 29] sl sts, 35 [36, 33, 30, 29, 30] hdc at end of last rnd)*

UPPER SLEEVE SHAPING

Rnd 1: Ch 2, [sl st in next hdc, hdc in next sl st] around, turn.

Rnd 2: Rep rnd 1.

Rnd 3: Ch 1, sl st dec in next hdc and next sl st, [sl st in next hdc, hdc in next sl st] around, join in sl st dec, turn. *(33 [34, 31, 28, 29, 28] sl sts, 34 [35, 32, 29, 28, 29] hdc)*

Rnd 4: Rep rnd 3. *(32 [33, 30, 27, 26, 27] sl sts, 33 [34, 31, 28, 27, 28] hdc)*

Next rnds: [Rep rnds 1–4 consecutively] 4 [4, 2, 0, 0, 1] time(s). *(24 [25, 26, 27, 26, 25] sl sts, 25 [26, 27, 28, 27, 26] hdc)*

LOWER SLEEVE SHAPING

Rnd 1: Ch 2, [sl st in next hdc, hdc in next sl st] across, turn.

Rnds 2–4: [Rep rnd 1] 3 times.

Rnd 5: Ch 1, sl st dec in next hdc and next sl st, [sl st in next hdc, hdc in next sl st] around, join in sl st dec, turn. *(23 [24, 25, 26, 27, 24] sl sts, 24 [25, 26, 27, 26, 25] hdc)*

Rnd 6: Rep rnd 5. *(22 [23, 24, 25, 24, 23] sl sts, 23 [24, 25, 26, 25, 24] hdc)*

Rnds 7–10: [Rep rnd 1] 4 times.

Rnds 11 & 12: Rep rnd 5 twice. *(20 [21, 22, 23, 22, 21] sl sts, 21 [22, 23, 24, 23, 22] hdc)*

Next rnds: [Rep rnds 7–12 consecutively] 2 [2, 2, 2, 1, 0] time(s). *(18 [19, 20, 21, 20, 21] sl sts, 19 [20, 21, 22, 21, 22] hdc)*

Next rnd: Ch 2, [sl st in next hdc, hdc in next sl st] across, **do not turn.**

CUFF

Rnd 1: Ch 1, **sc dec* (see Stitch Guide) in next 2 sts, [dc in next st, sc in next st] twice, dc in next st, rep from * 5 times, [sc in next st, dc in next st] across, leaving last st unworked, join in beg sc dec. *(15 [16, 17, 18, 19, 20] sc, 15 [16, 17, 18, 19, 20] dc)*

Rnd 2: Ch 1, [sc in next sc, fpdc around next dc] around, join in beg sc. *(15 [16, 17, 18, 19, 20] sc, 15 [16, 17, 18, 19, 20] fpdc)*

Rnd 3: Ch 1, [sc in next sc, fpdc around next fpdc] around, join in beg sc.

Next rnds: Rep last rnd 3 [3, 3, 4, 4, 4] times.

TRIM

Rnd 1: Ch 1, **reverse sc** (see Stitch Guide) in each st around, join in beg reverse sc. Fasten off. *(28 [30, 32, 34, 36, 38] reverse sc)*

COLLAR

Row 1: With WS of Left Front facing, working in sts and rows at neck edge, sk first 4 rows, join in next sp, sc in same sp, [dc in next sp, sc in next sp] around neck edge, ending sc in 4th row from outer edge of Right Front, turn. *(26 [26, 26, 33, 33, 33] sc, 25 [25, 25, 32, 32, 32] dc)*

Row 2: Ch 1, sc in each st across, turn. *(51 [51, 51, 65, 65, 65] sc)*

Row 3: Ch 1, sc in first sc, ◊sk next sc, fpdc around next dc 2 rows below, sk sc on this row behind fpdc, sc in next sc◊, *[fpdc around next dc 2 rows below, sk sc on this row behind fpdc, sc in next sc, fpdc around same sc, sc in next sc] twice*, rep between ◊ 3 [3, 3, 5, 5, 5] times, rep between * once, rep between ◊ 9 [9, 9, 13, 13, 13] times, rep between * once, rep between ◊ 3 [3, 3, 5, 5, 5] times, rep between * once, rep between ◊ once, turn.

Row 4: Rep row 2. *(67 [67, 67, 83, 83, 83] sc)*

Row 5: Ch 1, sc in first sc, [sk next sc, fpdc around fpdc 2 rows below, sc in next sc] across, turn.

Next rows: [Rep rows 4 and 5 alternately] 5 [5, 5, 6, 6, 6] times. At end of last row, fasten off.

POCKET WELT
Row 1: With RS facing, working on Pocket Opening edge closest to center front, join with sc in first st, [dc in next st, sc in next st] across, turn. *(10 sc, 9 dc)*

Row 2: Ch 1, sc in each st across, turn. *(19 sc)*

Row 3: Ch 1, [sc in next sc, sk next sc, fpdc around next dc in row before last] across, sc in last sc. Fasten off. *(10 sc, 9 fpdc)*

Rep instructions on 2nd Pocket.

POCKET SACK
Row 1: With RS of Pocket Opening edge closer to side, join in first st, ch 1, 2 **ext sc** *(see Special Stitch)* in same st, ext sc in each st across, ending with 2 ext sc in last st, turn. *(21 ext sc)*

Rows 2–23: Ch 1, ext sc in each ext sc, across, turn.

Row 24: Ch 1, sk first ext sc, ext sc in each ext sc, across, turn. *(20 ext sc)*

Row 25: Rep row 24. Fasten off. *(19 ext sc)*

Rep instructions for 2nd Pocket.

FINISHING
Sew left side seam.

On WS, sew free end of each Pocket Sack to first row of each Welt.

Sew edges of Pocket Sacks closed.

Sew side edges of Pocket Welts in place.

Sew buttons to Left Front using Buttonholes in Right Front as guide.

TRIM
Working in starting ch on opposite side of rnd 1 on Right Cuff, join on RS in first ch, ch 1, reverse sc in each ch around, join in beg reverse sc. Fasten off. *(28 [30, 32, 34, 36, 38] reverse sc)*

Rep Trim on other Sleeve.

Working in sts and ends of rows, join on RS at Left side seam, ch 1, reverse sc evenly around all outer edges, join in beg reverse sc. Fasten off. ■

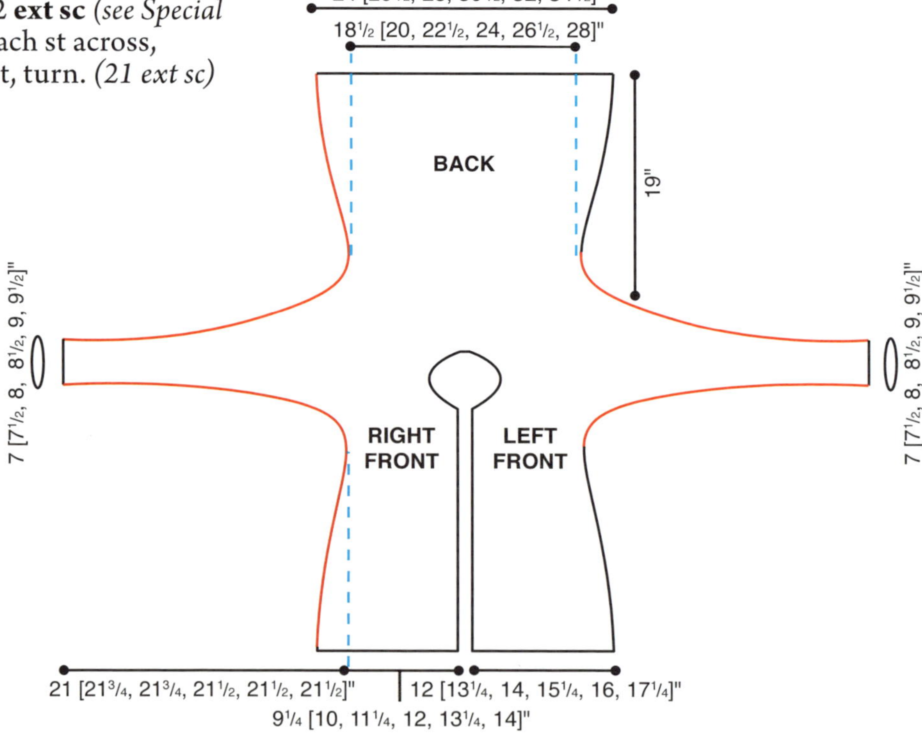

Red lines indicate edges that are crocheted together as work progresses

Cable Car **Coat**

SKILL LEVEL

INTERMEDIATE

FINISHED SIZES
Instructions given fit size small; changes for
medium, large, X-large, 2X-large and 3X-large
are in [ ].

FINISHED GARMENT MEASUREMENTS
Bust: 36 inches (*small*) [40 inches (*medium*),
44 inches (*large*), 48 inches (*X-large*),
52 inches (*2X-large*), 56 inches (*3X-large*)]

MATERIALS
- Red Heart Super Saver medium
  (worsted) weight yarn (5 oz/
  260 yds/141g per skein):
    8 [9, 10, 11, 12, 13] skeins
      #4334 buff fleck
- Size J/10/6mm crochet hook
  or size needed to obtain gauge
- Tapestry needle
- Sewing needle
- Matching sewing thread
- 7/8-inch buttons: 4

GAUGE
Bottom cables: 12 sts = 4 inches; 11 rows =
4 inches
Waist hdc rib: 12 sts = 3½ inches; 4 rows =
1¾ inches
Bodice hdc: 12 sts = 4 inches; 10 rows = 4 inches
Take time to check gauge.

PATTERN NOTES
Join with slip stitch as indicated unless
otherwise stated.

Chain-2 at beginning of row or round
counts as first half double crochet unless
otherwise stated.

For bodice, sleeves and collar, each half double
crochet is made in the space between 2 half
double crochet in the row below.

SPECIAL STITCHES
Extended single crochet (ext sc): Insert hook
in place indicated, yo, pull lp through, yo,
pull through 1 lp on hook (*first step*), yo,
pull through 2 lps on hook.

Extended single crochet decrease (ext sc dec): [Insert hook in place indicated, yo, pull lp through] twice, [yo, pull through 2 lps on hook] twice.

Cable: *Sk next ext sc, **fptr** (*see Stitch Guide*) around st 2 rows below sk ext sc*, ext sc in next ext sc, rep between * once.

Crossed Cable: Sk next 2 ext sc, fptr around fptr 2 rows below next ext sc, working behind fptr just worked, sk next ext sc, ext sc in next ext sc, crossing over fptr just made, fptr in fptr 2 rows below first sk ext sc, sk next ext sc behind fptr just worked.

INSTRUCTIONS
COAT
BACK

Row 1 (RS): Ch 2, **ext sc** (*see Special Stitches*) in 2nd ch from hook, ext sc in first step of last ext sc 69 [74, 83, 90, 97, 106] times, turn. (*70 [75, 84, 91, 98, 107] ext sc*)

Row 2: Ch 1, ext sc in each ext sc across, turn.

Row 3: Ch 1, ext sc in each of first 2 [1, 2, 4, 2, 4] ext sc, ***cable** (*see Special Stitches*), ext sc in each of next 4 [4, 4, 5, 4, 5] ext sc, rep from * 8 [9, 10, 9, 12, 11] times, cable, ext sc in each of last 2 [1, 2, 4, 2, 4] ext sc, turn. (*50 [53, 60, 69, 70, 81] ext sc, 20 [22, 24, 22, 28, 26] fptr*)

Row 4: Ch 1, ext sc in each ext sc across, turn. (*70 [75, 84, 91, 98, 107] ext sc*)

Row 5: Ch 1, ext sc in each of first 2 [1, 2, 4, 2, 4] ext sc, [**crossed cable** (*see Special Stitches*), ext sc in each of next 4 [4, 4, 5, 4, 5] ext sc] 9 [10, 11, 10, 13, 12] times, crossed cable, ext sc in each of last 2 [1, 2, 4, 2, 4] ext sc, turn. (*50 [53, 60, 69, 70, 81] ext sc, 20 [22, 24, 22, 28, 26] fptr*)

Rows 6–21: [Rep rows 2–5 consecutively] 4 times.

Row 22: Ch 1, ext sc in each of first 6 [4, 6, 9, 5, 9] ext sc, ***ext sc dec** (*see Special Stitches*) in next 2 ext sc, ext sc in each of next 5 [5, 5, 6, 5, 6] ext sc, rep from * 8 [9, 10, 9, 12, 11] times, ext sc in last 1 [1, 1, 2, 2, 2] ext sc, turn. (*61 [65, 73, 81, 85, 95] ext sc*)

Row 23: Ch 1, ext sc in each of first 2 [1, 2, 4, 2, 4] ext sc, *cable, ext sc in each of next 3 [3, 3, 4, 3, 4] ext sc, rep from * 8 [9, 10, 9, 12, 11] times, cable, ext sc in each of last 2 [1, 2, 4, 2, 4] ext sc, turn. *(41 [43, 49, 59, 57, 69] ext sc, 20 [22, 24, 22, 28, 26] fptr)*

Row 24: Ch 1, ext sc in each st across, turn. *(61 [65, 73, 81, 85, 95] ext sc)*

Row 25: Ch 1, ext sc in each of first 2 [1, 2, 4, 2, 4] ext sc, *crossed cable, ext sc in each of next 3 [3, 3, 4, 3, 4] ext sc, rep from * 8 [9, 10, 9, 12, 11] times, crossed cable, ext sc in each of last 2 [1, 2, 4, 2, 4] ext sc, turn. *(41 [43, 49, 59, 57, 69] ext sc, 20 [22, 24, 22, 28, 26] fptr)*

Row 26: Ch 1, ext sc in each st across, turn.

Next rows: [Rep rows 23–26 consecutively] 1 [1, 1, 2, 2, 2] time(s).

Next rows: Rep rows 23–25 once.

HIP SHAPING

Row 1: Ch 1, *ext sc in each of first 5 [10, 10, 10, 15, 10] sts*, ◊[ext sc dec in next 2 sts, ext sc in each of next 4 sts] 3 [2, 3, 4, 3, 5] times, ext sc dec in next 2 sts◊, ext sc in each of next 11 [17, 13, 9, 15, 11] ext sc, rep between ◊ once, rep between * once, turn. *(53 [59, 65, 71, 77, 83] ext sc)*

Row 2: Ch 1, ext sc in each of first 2 [1, 2, 4, 2, 4] ext sc, [◊cable, ext sc in each of next 3 ext sc◊] 0 [1, 1, 0, 1, 0] time(s), *cable, ext sc in each of next 2 [2, 2, 3, 2, 3] ext sc, rep from * 3 [2, 3, 9, 3, 11] times**, rep between ◊ 1 [2, 1, 0, 3, 0] time(s), rep from * to ** 1 [1, 1, 0, 1, 0] time(s), rep between ◊ 0 [1, 1, 0, 1, 0] time(s), cable, ext sc in each of last 2 [1, 2, 4, 2, 4] ext sc, turn. *(33 [37, 41, 49, 49, 57] ext sc, 20 [22, 24, 22, 28, 26] fptr)*

Row 3: Ch 1, ext sc in each st across, turn. *(53 [59, 65, 71, 77, 83] ext sc)*

Row 4: Ch 1, ext sc in each of first 2 [1, 2, 4, 2, 4] ext sc, [◊crossed cable, ext sc in each of next 3 ext sc◊] 0 [1, 1, 0, 1, 0] time(s), *crossed cable, ext sc in each of next 2 [2, 2, 3, 2, 3] ext sc, rep from * 3 [2, 3, 9, 3, 11] times**, rep between ◊ 1 [2, 1, 0, 3, 0] time(s), rep from * to ** 1 [1, 1, 0, 1, 0] time, rep between ◊ 0 [1, 1, 0, 1, 0] time,

crossed cable, ext sc in each of last 2 [1, 2, 4, 2, 4] ext sc, turn. *(33 [37, 41, 49, 49, 57] ext sc, 20 [22, 24, 22, 28, 26] fptr)*

Row 5: Ch 1, ext sc in each st across, turn. *(53 [59, 65, 71, 77, 83] ext sc)*

Row 6: Rep row 2.

WAIST SHAPING

Row 1: Sl st in each st across, sl st in beg ch-1, turn. *(54 [60, 66, 72, 78, 84] sl sts)*

Row 2 (RS): **Ch 2** *(see Pattern Notes)*, hdc in **front lp** *(see Stitch Guide)* of each sl st across, turn. *(54 [60, 66, 72, 78, 84] hdc)*

Row 3: Ch 2, hdc in **front bar** *(see illustration)* of each hdc, turn.

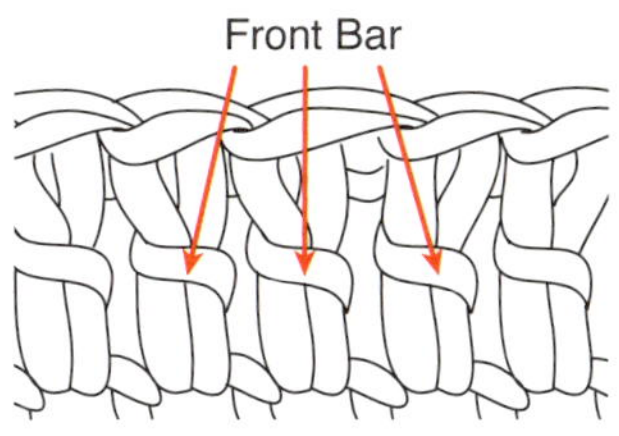

Front Bar of Half Double Crochet

Row 4: Ch 2, hdc in **back lp** *(see Stitch Guide)* of each hdc, turn.

Next rows: [Rep rows 3 and 4] 0 [0, 0, 1, 1, 1] time(s).

Next row: Rep row 3.

BODICE

Row 1: (RS): Ch 2, [hdc in sp between next 2 hdc] across, ending with hdc in sp between last hdc and beg ch, turn.

Next rows: Rep last row 16 [16, 14, 12, 12, 12] times.

ARMHOLE SHAPING

Row 1 (RS): Ch 1, sl st in each of first 2 [2, 2, 4, 4, 4] hdc, ch 1, **hdc dec** *(see Stitch Guide)* in next 2 sps between hdc, [hdc in sp between next 2 hdc] across until 4 [4, 4, 6, 6, 6] sps rem, hdc dec in next 2 sps, leaving rem sps unworked, turn. *(48 [54, 60, 62, 68, 74] hdc)*

Row 2: Ch 2, hdc dec in first 2 sps, [hdc in sp between next 2 hdc] across until 2 sps rem, hdc dec in last 2 sps, turn. *(46 [52, 58, 60, 66, 72] hdc)*

Rows 3 & 4: Rep row 2. *(42 [48, 54, 56, 62, 68] hdc at end of last row)*

Row 5: Ch 2, [hdc in sp between next 2 hdc] across, ending with hdc in sp between last hdc and beg ch, turn.

Next rows: [Rep row 2] 1 [3, 5, 5, 7, 9] time(s). *(40 [42, 44, 46, 48, 50] hdc)*

Next rows: [Rep row 5] 10 [10, 10, 8, 8, 6] times.

LEFT SHOULDER
Row 1: Ch 2, [hdc in sp between next 2 hdc] 12 [12, 14, 14, 16, 16] times, hdc dec in next 2 sps, leaving rem sts unworked, turn. *(14 [14, 16, 16, 18, 18] hdc)*

Row 2: Ch 2, hdc dec in first 2 sps, [hdc in sp between next 2 hdc] 4 [4, 5, 5, 6, 6] times, hdc dec in next 2 sps, leaving rem sts unworked, turn. *(7 [7, 8, 8, 9, 9] hdc)*

Row 3: Ch 1, hdc dec in first 2 sps, [hdc in sp between next 2 hdc] across, ending hdc in sp between last hdc and beg ch, turn. *(6 [6, 7, 7, 8, 8] hdc)*

Row 4: Ch 2, [hdc in sp between next 2 hdc] 5 [5, 6, 6, 7, 7] times, hdc in end of next row 2 rows below, hdc in next sp 3 rows below, hdc in each sp across, ending with hdc in sp between last hdc and beg ch. *(12 [12, 14, 14, 16, 16] hdc)*

SMALL, MEDIUM & LARGE SIZES ONLY
Fasten off.

X-LARGE, 2X-LARGE & 3X-LARGE SIZES ONLY
Row [5]: Ch 2, [hdc in sp between next 2 hdc] across, ending with hdc in sp between last hdc and beg ch, turn.

Row [6]: Rep row 5. Fasten off.

RIGHT SHOULDER
Row 1: With WS of Back facing, sk next 10 [12, 12, 14, 12, 14] sps, **join** *(see Pattern Notes)* in next sp, ch 2, [hdc in sp between next 2 hdc] across, ending with hdc in sp between last hdc and beg ch, turn. *(14 [14, 16, 16, 18, 18] hdc)*

Row 2: Ch 2, [hdc in sp between next 2 hdc] across until 2 sps rem, hdc dec in last 2 sps, turn. *(13 [13, 15, 15, 17, 17] hdc)*

Row 3: Ch 2, hdc dec in first 2 sps, [hdc in sp between next 2 hdc] 4 [4, 5, 5, 6, 6] times, hdc dec in next 2 sps, leaving rem sps unworked, turn. *(7 [7, 8, 8, 9, 9] hdc)*

Row 4: Ch 1, hdc dec in first 2 sps, [hdc in sp between next 2 hdc] across, ending with hdc in sp between last hdc and beg ch, turn. *(6 [6, 7, 7, 8, 8] hdc)*

SMALL, MEDIUM & LARGE SIZES ONLY
Fasten off.

X-LARGE, 2X-LARGE & 3X-LARGE SIZES ONLY
Row [5]: Ch 2, [hdc in sp between next 2 hdc] [6, 7, 7] times, hdc in end of row 2 rows below, hdc in next sp 3 rows below, hdc in each sp across, ending with hdc in sp between last hdc and beg ch, turn. *([14, 16, 16] hdc)*

Row [6]: Ch 2, [hdc in sp between next 2 hdc] across, ending with hdc in sp between last hdc and beg ch, turn.

LEFT FRONT
Row 1(RS): Ch 2, ext sc in 2nd ch from hook, [ext sc in first step of last ext sc] 34 [37, 42, 45, 49, 53] times, turn. *(35 [38, 43, 46, 50, 54] ext sc)*

Row 2: Ch 1, ext sc in each ext sc across, turn.

Row 3: Ch 1, ext sc in each of first 2 [3, 2, 1, 2, 1] ext sc, *cable, ext sc in each of next 4 [4, 4, 5, 4, 5] ext sc, rep from * 3 [3, 4, 4, 5, 5] times, cable, ext sc in each of last 2 [4, 3, 2, 3, 2] ext sc, turn. *(25 [28, 31, 34, 36, 40] ext sc, 10 [10, 12, 12, 14, 14] fptr)*

Row 4: Ch 1, ext sc in each st across, turn. *(35 [38, 43, 46, 50, 54] ext sc)*

Row 5: Ch 1, ext sc in each of first 2 [3, 2, 1, 2, 1] ext sc, *crossed cable, ext sc in each of next 4 [4, 4, 5, 4, 5] ext sc, rep from * 3 [3, 4, 4, 5, 5] times, crossed cable, ext sc in each of last 2 [4, 3, 2, 3, 2] ext sc, turn. *(25 [28, 31, 34, 36, 40] ext sc, 10 [10, 12, 12, 14, 14] fptr)*

Rows 6–21: [Rep rows 2–5 consecutively] 4 times.

Row 22: Ch 1, ext sc in each of first 6 [7, 6, 5, 6, 5] ext sc, *ext sc dec in next 2 ext sc, ext sc in each of next 5 [5, 5, 6, 5, 6] ext sc, rep from * 3 [3, 4, 4, 5, 5] times, ext sc in each of last 1 [3, 2, 1, 2, 1] ext sc, turn. *(31 [34, 38, 41, 44, 48] ext sc)*

Row 23: Ch 1, ext sc in each of first 2 [3, 2, 1, 2, 1] ext sc, *cable, ext sc in each of next 3 [3, 3, 4, 3, 4] ext sc, rep from * 3 [3, 4, 4, 5, 5] times, cable, ext sc in each of last 2 [4, 3, 2, 3, 2] ext sc, turn. *(21 [24, 26, 29, 30, 34] ext sc, 10 [10, 12, 12, 14, 14] fptr)*

Row 24: Ch 1, ext sc in each st across, turn. *(31 [34, 38, 41, 44, 48] ext sc)*

Row 25: Ch 1, ext sc in each of first 2 [3, 2, 1, 2, 1] ext sc, *crossed cable, ext sc in next 3 [3, 3, 4, 3, 4] ext sc, rep from * 3 [3, 4, 4, 5, 5] times, crossed cable, ext sc in each of last 2 [4, 3, 2, 3, 2] ext sc, turn. *(21 [24, 26, 29, 30, 34] ext sc, 10 [10, 12, 12, 14, 14] fptr)*

Row 26: Ch 1, ext sc in each st across, turn.

Next rows: [Rep rows 23–26 consecutively] 1 [1, 1, 2, 2, 2] time(s).

Next rows: [Rep rows 23–25] once.

HIP SHAPING

Row 1: Ch 1, ext sc in each of first 6 [7, 6, 5, 6, 5] ext sc, *ext sc dec in next 2 ext sc, ext sc in each of next 4 [4, 4, 5, 4, 5] ext sc, rep from * 3 [3, 4, 4, 5, 5] times, ext sc in each of last 1 [3, 2, 1, 2, 1] ext sc, turn. *(27 [30, 33, 36, 38, 42] ext sc)*

Row 2: Ch 1, ext sc in each of first 2 [3, 2, 1, 2, 1] ext sc, *cable, ext sc in each of next 2 [2, 2, 3, 2, 3] ext sc, rep from * 3 [3, 4, 4, 5, 5] times, cable, ext sc in each of last 2 [4, 3, 2, 3, 2] ext sc, turn. *(17 [20, 21, 24, 24, 28] ext sc, 10 [10, 12, 12, 14, 14] fptr)*

Row 3: Ch 1, ext sc in each st across, turn. *(27 [30, 33, 36, 38, 42] ext sc)*

Row 4: Ch 1, ext sc in each of first 2 [3, 2, 1, 2, 1] ext sc, *crossed cable, ext sc in each of next 2 [2, 2, 3, 2, 3] ext sc, rep from * 3 [3, 4, 4, 5, 5] times, crossed cable, ext sc in each of last 2 [4, 3, 2, 3, 2] ext sc, turn. *(17 [20, 21, 24, 24, 28] ext sc, 10 [10, 12, 12, 14, 14] fptr)*

Row 5: Ch 1, ext sc in each st across, turn. *(27 [30, 33, 36, 36, 42] ext sc)*

Row 6: Rep row 2.

WAIST SHAPING
Row 1: Sl st in each st across, turn. *(27 [30, 33, 36, 38, 42] sl sts)*

Row 2 (RS): Ch 2, hdc in front lp of each sl st across, turn. *(27 [30, 33, 36, 38, 42] hdc)*

Row 3: Ch 2, hdc in front bar of each hdc, turn.

Row 4: Ch 2, hdc in back lp of each hdc, turn.

Next rows: [Rep rows 3 and 4] 0 [0, 0, 1, 1, 1] time.

Next row: Rep row 3.

BODICE
Row 1 (RS): Ch 2, [hdc in sp between next 2 hdc] across, ending with hdc in sp between last hdc and beg ch, turn.

Next rows: Rep last row 16 [16, 14, 12, 12, 12] times.

ARMHOLE SHAPING
Row 1 (RS): Ch 2, [hdc in sp between next 2 hdc] across until 4 [4, 4, 6, 5, 6] sps rem, hdc dec in next 2 sps, leaving rem sps unworked, turn. *(24 [27, 30, 31, 34, 37] hdc)*

Row 2: Ch 2, hdc dec in first 2 sps, [hdc in sp between next 2 hdc] across, ending with hdc in sp between last hdc and beg ch, turn. *(23 [26, 29, 30, 33, 36] hdc)*

Row 3: Ch 2, [hdc in sp between next 2 hdc] across to last 2 sps rem, hdc dec in last 2 sps, turn. *(22 [25, 28, 29, 32, 35] hdc)*

Row 4: Rep row 2. *(21 [24, 27, 28, 31, 34] hdc)*

Row 5: Ch 2, [hdc in sp between next 2 hdc] across, ending with hdc in sp between last hdc and beg ch, turn.

Next rows: [Rep rows 2 and 3 alternately] 0 [1, 2, 2, 3, 4] time(s). *(21 [22, 23, 24, 25, 26] hdc at end of last row)*

Next row: Rep row 2. *(20 [21, 22, 23, 24, 25] hdc)*

Next rows: [Rep row 5] 6 [6, 6, 4, 4, 2] times.

NECKLINE

Row 1: Ch 1, sl st in each of first 4 [5, 4, 5, 4, 5] hdc, ch 2, hdc dec in next 2 sps, [hdc in sp between next 2 hdc] across, ending with hdc in sp between last hdc and beg ch, turn. *(16 [16, 18, 18, 20, 20] hdc)*

Row 2: Ch 2, [hdc in sp between next 2 hdc] across to last 2 sps rem, hdc dec in last 2 sps, turn. *(15 [15, 17, 17, 19, 19] hdc)*

Row 3: Ch 2, hdc dec in first 2 sps, [hdc in sp between next 2 hdc] across, ending with hdc in sp between last hdc and beg ch, turn. *(14 [14, 16, 16, 18, 18] hdc)*

Rows 4 & 5: Rep rows 2 and 3. *(12 [12, 14, 14, 16, 16] hdc at end of last row)*

Row 6: Ch 2, [hdc in sp between next 2 hdc] across, ending with hdc in sp between last hdc and beg ch, turn.

Next rows: [Rep row 6] 0 [0, 0, 2, 2, 2] times.

Next row: [Hdc in sp between next 2 hdc] 6 [6, 7, 7, 8, 8] times, hdc dec in next 2 sps, turn. *(7 [7, 8, 8, 9, 9] hdc)*

Next row: Ch 1, hdc dec in first 2 sps, [hdc in sp between next 2 hdc] across, ending with hdc in sp between last hdc and beg ch. Fasten off. *(5 [5, 6, 6, 7, 7] hdc)*

RIGHT FRONT

Row 1 (RS): Ch 2, ext sc in 2nd ch from hook, [ext sc in first step of last ext sc] 34 [37, 42, 45, 49, 53] times, turn. *(35 [38, 43, 46, 50, 54] ext sc)*

Row 2: Ch 1, ext sc in each ext sc across, turn.

Row 3: Ch 1, ext sc in each of first 2 [4, 3, 2, 3, 2] ext sc, *cable, ext sc in each of next 4 [4, 4, 5, 4, 5] ext sc, rep from * 3 [3, 4, 4, 5, 5] times, cable, ext sc in each of last 2 [3, 2, 1, 2, 1] ext sc, turn. *(25 [28, 31, 34, 36, 40] ext sc, 10 [10, 12, 12, 14, 14] fptr)*

Row 4: Ch 1, ext sc in each st across, turn. *(35 [38, 43, 46, 50, 54] ext sc)*

Row 5: Ch 1, ext sc in each of first 2 [4, 3, 2, 3, 2] ext sc, *crossed cable, ext sc in each of next 4 [4, 4, 5, 4, 5] ext sc, rep from * 3 [3, 4, 4, 5, 5] times, crossed cable, ext sc in each of last 2 [3, 2, 1, 2, 1] ext sc, turn. *(25 [28, 31, 34, 36, 40] ext sc, 10 [10, 12, 12, 14, 14] fptr)*

Rows 6–21: [Rep rows 2–5 consecutively] 4 times.

Row 22: Ch 1, ext sc in each of first 6 [7, 6, 5, 6, 5] ext sc, *ext sc dec in next 2 ext sc, ext sc in each of next 5 [5, 5, 6, 5, 6] ext sc, rep from * 3 [3, 4, 4, 5, 5] times, ext sc in each of last 1 [3, 2, 1, 2, 1] ext sc, turn. *(31 [34, 38, 41, 44, 48] ext sc)*

Row 23: Ch 1, ext sc in each of first 2 [4, 3, 2, 3, 2] ext sc, *cable, ext sc in each of next 3 [3, 3, 4, 3, 4] ext sc, rep from * 3 [3, 4, 4, 5, 5] times, cable, ext sc in each of last 2 [3, 2, 1, 2, 1] ext sc, turn. *(21 [24, 26, 29, 30, 34] ext sc, 10 [10, 12, 12, 14, 14] fptr)*

Row 24: Ch 1, ext sc in each st across, turn. *(31 [34, 38, 41, 44, 48] ext sc)*

Row 25: Ch 1, ext sc in each of first 2 [4, 3, 2, 3, 2] ext sc, *crossed cable, ext sc in each of next 3 [3, 3, 4, 3, 4] ext sc, rep from * 3 [3, 4, 4, 5, 5] times, crossed cable, ext sc in each of last 2 [3, 2, 1, 2, 1] ext sc, turn. *(21 [24, 26, 29, 30, 34] ext sc, 10 [10, 12, 12, 14, 14] fptr)*

Row 26: Ch 1, ext sc in each st across, turn.

Next rows: [Rep rows 23–26 consecutively] 1 [1, 1, 2, 2, 2] time(s).

Next rows: [Rep rows 23–25] once.

HIP SHAPING
Row 1: Ch 1, ext sc in each of first 6 [7, 6, 5, 6, 5] ext sc, *ext sc dec in next 2 ext sc, ext sc in each of next 4 [4, 4, 5, 4, 5] ext sc, rep from * 3 [3, 4, 4, 5, 5] times, ext sc in each of last 1 [3, 2, 1, 2, 1] ext sc, turn. (27 [30, 33, 36, 38, 42] ext sc)

Row 2: Ch 1, ext sc in each of first 2 [4, 3, 2, 3, 2] ext sc, *cable, ext sc in each of next 2 [2, 2, 3, 2, 3] ext sc, rep from * 3 [3, 4, 4, 5, 5] times, cable, ext sc in each of last 2 [3, 2, 1, 2, 1] ext sc, turn. (17 [20, 21, 24, 24, 28] ext sc, 10 [10, 12, 12, 14, 14] fptr)

Row 3: Ch 1, ext sc in each st across, turn. (27 [30, 33, 36, 38, 42] ext sc)

Row 4: Ch 1, ext sc in each of first 2 [4, 3, 2, 3, 2] ext sc, *crossed cable, ext sc in each of next 2 [2, 2, 3, 2, 3] ext sc, rep from * 3 [3, 4, 4, 5, 5] times, crossed cable, ext sc in each of last 2 [3, 2, 1, 2, 1] ext sc, turn. (17 [20, 21, 24, 24, 28] ext sc, 10 [10, 12, 12, 14, 14] fptr)

Row 5: Ch 1, ext sc in each st across, turn. (27 [30, 33, 36, 38, 42] ext sc)

Row 6: Rep row 2.

WAIST SHAPING
Rep instructions for Waist Shaping of Left Front.

BODICE
Rep instructions for Bodice of Left Front.

ARMHOLE SHAPING
Row 1 (RS): Ch 1, sl st in each of first 3 [3, 3, 5, 4, 5] hdc, ch 1, hdc dec in next 2 sps, [hdc in sp between next 2 hdc] across, turn. (24 [27, 30, 31, 34, 37] hdc)

Row 2: Ch 2, [hdc in sp between next 2 hdc] across to last 2 sps rem, hdc dec in last 2 sps, turn. (23 [26, 29, 30, 33, 36] hdc)

Row 3: Ch 2, hdc dec in first 2 sps, [hdc in sp between next 2 hdc] across, ending with hdc in sp between last hdc and beg ch, turn. (22 [25, 28, 29, 32, 35] hdc)

Row 4: Rep row 2. (21 [24, 27, 28, 31, 34] hdc)

Row 5: Ch 2, [hdc in sp between next 2 hdc] across, ending with hdc in sp between last hdc and beg ch, turn.

Next rows: [Rep rows 2 and 3 alternately] 0 [1, 2, 2, 3, 4] time(s). (21 [22, 23, 24, 25, 26] hdc)

Next row: Rep row 2. (20 [21, 22, 23, 24, 25] hdc)

Next rows: [Rep row 5] 6 [6, 6, 4, 4, 2] times.

NECKLINE
Row 1: [Hdc in sp between next 2 hdc] across to last 5 [6, 5, 6, 5, 6] sps rem, hdc dec in next 2 sps, leaving rem sps unworked, turn. (16 [16, 18, 18, 20, 20] hdc)

Row 2: Ch 2, hdc dec in first 2 sps, [hdc in sp between next 2 hdc] across, ending with hdc in sp between last hdc and beg ch, turn. (15 [15, 17, 17, 19, 19] hdc)

Row 3: Ch 2, [hdc in sp between next 2 hdc] across to last 2 sps rem, hdc dec in last 2 sps, turn. (14 [14, 16, 16, 18, 18] hdc)

Rows 4 & 5: Rep rows 2 and 3. (12 [12, 14, 14, 16, 16] hdc at end of last row)

Row 6: [Hdc in sp between next 2 hdc] 6 [6, 7, 7, 8, 8] times, hdc dec in next 2 sps, leaving rem sps unworked, turn. (7 [7, 8, 8, 9, 9] hdc)

Row 7: Ch 1, hdc dec in first 2 sps, [hdc in sp between next 2 hdc] across, ending with hdc in sp between last hdc and beg ch, turn. (5 [5, 6, 6, 7, 7] hdc)

Row 8: Ch 2, [hdc in sp between next 2 hdc] 5 [5, 6, 6, 7, 7] times, hdc in sp 2 rows below, hdc in next sp 3 rows below, [hdc in sp between next 2 hdc] across, ending with hdc in sp between last hdc and beg ch, turn. (12 [12, 14, 14, 16, 16] hdc)

SMALL, MEDIUM & LARGE SIZES ONLY
Fasten off.

X-LARGE, 2X-LARGE & 3X-LARGE SIZES ONLY
Row [9]: Ch 2, [hdc in sp between next 2 hdc] across, ending with hdc in sp between last hdc and beg ch, turn.

Row [10]: Rep row 9. Fasten off.

SLEEVE
MAKE 2.
Row 1 (RS): Ch 27 [29, 31, 33, 35, 39], hdc in 3rd ch from hook (*first 2 chs count as first hdc*) and in each ch across, turn. (*26 [28, 30, 32, 34, 38] hdc*)

Row 2: Ch 2, [hdc in sp between next 2 hdc] across, ending with hdc in sp between last hdc and beg ch, turn.

Row 3: Ch 2, [hdc in sp between next 2 hdc] across, hdc in sp between last hdc and beg ch, hdc in beg ch, turn. (*27 [29, 31, 33, 35, 39] hdc*)

Row 4: Rep row 3. (*28 [30, 32, 34, 36, 40] hdc*)

Next rows: [Rep row 2] 3 [3, 3, 1, 1, 1] time(s).

Next rows: [Rep last 5 [5, 5, 3, 3, 3] rows] 6 [6, 7, 12, 13, 13] times. (*40 [42, 46, 58, 62, 66] hdc at end of last row*)

Next rows: [Rep row 2] 6 [6, 1, 3, 0, 0] time(s).

CAP SHAPING
Row 1: Ch 1, sl st in each of first 3 [2, 1, 5, 5, 6] hdc, ch 2, hdc dec in next 2 sps, [hdc in sp between next 2 hdc] across to last 6 [5, 4, 8, 8, 9] sps, hdc dec in next 2 sps, leaving rem sps unworked, turn. (*32 [36, 42, 46, 50, 52] hdc*)

Row 2: Ch 2, hdc dec in next 2 sps, [hdc in sp between next 2 hdc] across to last 2 sps rem, hdc dec in last 2 sps, turn. (*30 [34, 40, 44, 48, 50] hdc*)

Next rows: Rep last row 9 [11, 13, 15, 17, 17] times. At end of last row, fasten off. (*12 [12, 14, 14, 14, 16] hdc at end of last row*)

ASSEMBLY
Sew shoulder seams.

Fold 1 Sleeve in half lengthwise, place fold at shoulder seam and sew in place.

Rep with rem Sleeve.

Sew side and Sleeve seams.

COLLAR

Row 1: Working around neck edge in sts and ends of rows, with WS of Left Front facing, join in first hdc, ch 2, [hdc in sp between next 2 hdc] 3 [4, 3, 4, 3, 4] times, *[2 hdc in next row, hdc in next row] 6 [6, 6, 8, 8, 8] times*, [hdc in sp between next 2 hdc] 10 [12, 12, 14, 12, 14] times, rep between * once, [hdc in sp between next 2 hdc] 2 [3, 2, 3, 2, 3] times, ending with 2 hdc in sp between last hdc and beg ch, turn. *(54 [58, 56, 72, 68, 72] hdc)*

Row 2 (RS): Ch 2, *[hdc in sp between next 2 hdc] twice, 2 hdc in sp between next 2 hdc, rep from * across, ending with [hdc in sp between next 2 hdc] 2 [0, 1, 2, 1, 2] time(s), turn. *(71 [77, 74, 96, 90, 95] hdc)*

Row 3: Ch 2, [hdc in sp between next 2 hdc] across, ending with hdc in sp between last hdc and beg ch, turn.

Next rows: Rep last row 9 [9, 9, 11, 11, 11] times. At end of last row, fasten off.

TRIM

Row 1: With RS of Bodice facing, join at base of Collar on Left Front, working in ends of rows and sts, evenly sp sc around outer edges, working 3 sc in each corner and ending at base of Collar on Right Front, **do not turn.**

Row 2: Ch 1, working from left to right, **reverse sc** *(see Stitch Guide)* in each sc across. Fasten off.

COLLAR TRIM

Row 1: With WS of Collar facing, join at base of Collar on Left Front, working in ends of rows and sts, evenly sp sc around outer edges, working 3 sc in each corner and ending at base of Collar on Right Front, **do not turn.**

Row 2: Ch 1, working from left to right, reverse sc in each sc around. Fasten off.

SLEEVE TRIM

Rnd 1: With RS facing, working in starting ch on opposite side of row 1, join with sc in seam, sc in each ch around, join in beg sc, **do not turn.**

Rnd 2: Ch 1, working from left to right, reverse sc in each sc around, join in beg reverse sc. Fasten off.

FINISHING

Evenly sp buttons between neck waistband and sew buttons to Left Front, using sps between sts on Right Front as buttonholes. ■

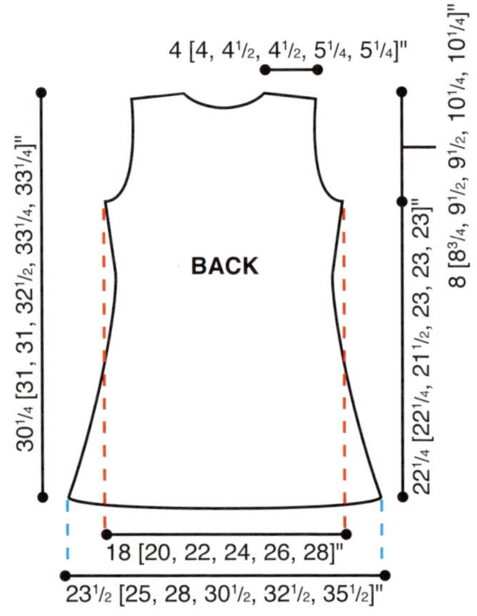

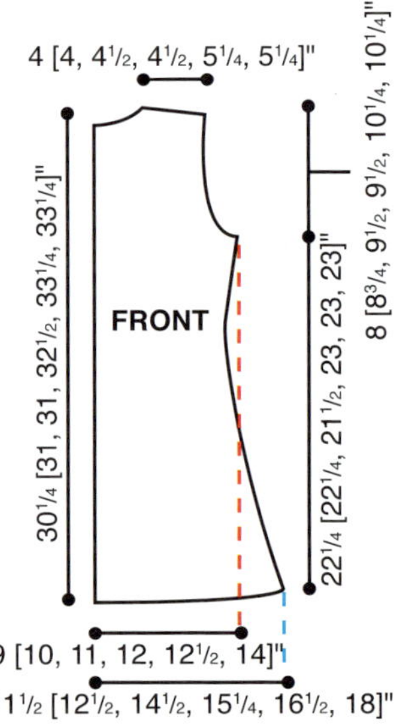

Chill Chaser **Coat**

SKILL LEVEL

INTERMEDIATE

FINISHED SIZES

Instructions given fit size small; changes for
medium, large, X-large, 2X-large and 3X-large
are in [ ].

FINISHED GARMENT MEASUREMENTS

Bust: 36 inches (*small*) [40 inches (*medium*),
44 inches (*large*), 48 inches (*X-large*),
52 inches (*2X-large*), 56 inches (*3X-large*)]

MATERIALS

- Red Heart Collage medium
  (worsted) weight yarn (3½ oz/
  218 yds/100g per skein):
    7 [7, 8, 9, 11, 11] skeins #2352
      crimson maple or #2940 wood trail
- Size J/10/6mm crochet hook
  or size needed to obtain gauge
- Tapestry needle
- Sewing needle
- Matching sewing thread
- ¾-inch buttons: 6
- Stitch markers

GAUGE

14 sts = 4 inches; 14 rows = 4 inches
Take time to check gauge.

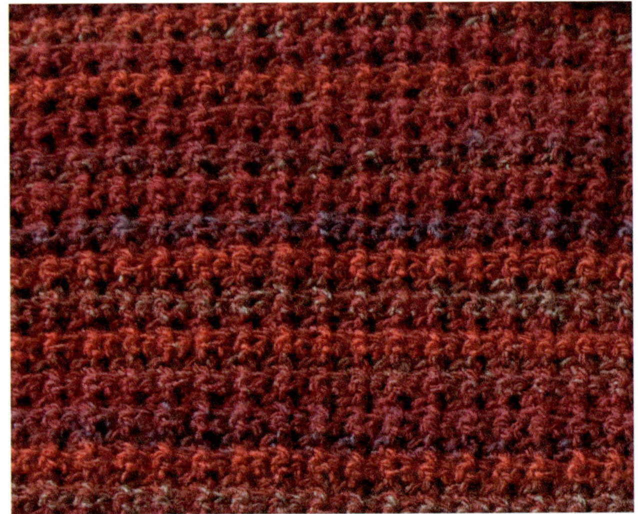

PATTERN NOTES

Sweater bottom is made first, from side to side.
  Remainder is worked into ends of rows and
  then split into 3 sections: Right and Left Fronts
  and Back.

Sleeves are worked together at underarm.
  Collar is crocheted directly onto neckline.

Join with slip stitch as indicated unless
  otherwise stated.

SPECIAL STITCH

Extended single crochet (ext sc): Insert hook
  in place indicated, yo, pull lp through, yo,
  pull through 1 lp on hook (*first step*), yo,
  pull through all lps on hook.

INSTRUCTIONS
JACKET
BOTTOM
Row 1: (WS): Ch 59 [61, 63, 65, 65, 67], sc in
2nd ch from hook and in each ch across, turn.
(58 [60, 62, 64, 64, 66] sc)

Row 2: (RS): Ch 1, sc in **back lp** *(see Stitch
Guide)* of first sc, sc in **front lp** *(see Stitch
Guide)* of next sc, [sc in back lp of next sc,
sc in front lp of next sc] across to last 8 sc,
sc in back lp of next st, sc in both lps of each
of last 7 sc, turn.

Row 3: Ch 1, sc in each of first 7 sc, *sc in back lp
of next sc**, sc in front lp of next sc, rep from *
across, ending last rep at **, turn.

Next rows: [Rep rows 2 and 3 alternately]
68 [75, 82, 89, 96, 103] times.

Last row: Rep row 2, **do not turn.**

BODICE
Row 1 (RS): Working in ends of rows, ch 1, sc
in each of first 2 [9, 2, 9, 3, 10] rows, **sc dec** *(see
Stitch Guide)* in next 2 rows, *sc in each of next
3 [3, 4, 4, 5, 5] rows, sc dec in next 2 rows, rep
from * 26 times, sc in last 1 [8, 2, 9, 2, 9] row(s),
turn. *(112 [126, 140, 154, 168, 182] sc)*

Row 2: Ch 1, sc in back lp of first st, sc in front lp of next st, [sc in back lp of next sc, sc in front lp of next sc] across, turn.

Row 3: Ch 1, sc in front lp of first st, sc in back lp of next st, [sc in front lp of next sc, sc in back lp of next sc] across, turn.

Next rows: [Rep rows 2 and 3 alternately] 4 [4, 3, 3, 2, 2] times.

Next row: Ch 1, sc in back lp of first st, sc in front lp of next st, *[sc in back lp of next sc, sc in front lp of next sc]* 2 [3, 3, 4, 4, 5] times, ◊**[sc in back lp of next sc, sc in front lp of same sc] twice**, rep between * 7 [8, 9, 10, 11, 12] times, rep from ◊ 5 times, rep between ** once, rep between * across, turn. (126 [140, 154, 168, 182, 196] sc)

Next row: Rep row 3.

Next rows: [Rep rows 2 and 3 alternately] 3 times.

UNDERARM SHAPING
Row 1: Ch 1, sc in back lp of first st, sc in front lp of next st, *[sc in back lp of next sc, sc in front lp of next sc]* 14 [16, 18, 19, 21, 23] times, **[sc in back lp of next sc, sc in front lp of same sc] twice**, rep between * 31 [34, 37, 42, 44, 48] times, rep between ** once, rep between * across, turn. (130 [144, 158, 172, 186, 200] sc)

Row 2: Ch 1, sc in front lp of first st, sc in back lp of next st, *[sc in front lp of next sc, sc in back lp of next sc]* 14 [16, 18, 20, 21, 23] times, **[sc in front lp of next sc, sc in back lp of same sc] twice**, rep between * 33 [36, 39, 42, 47, 50] times, rep between ** once, rep between * across, turn. (134 [148, 162, 176, 190, 204] sc)

Row 3: Ch 1, sc in back lp of first st, sc in front lp of next st, *[sc in back lp of next sc, sc in front lp of next sc]* 15 [17, 19, 20, 22, 24] times, **[sc in back lp of next sc, sc in front lp of same sc] twice**, rep between * 33 [36, 39, 44, 47, 50] times, rep between ** once, rep between * across, turn. (138 [152, 166, 180, 194, 208] sc)

Row 4: Ch 1, sc in front lp of first st, sc in back lp of next st, *[sc in front lp of next sc, sc in

back lp of next sc]* 16 [18, 20, 21, 23, 25] times, **[sc in front lp of next sc, sc in back lp of same sc] twice**, rep between * 33 [36, 39, 44, 47, 50] times, rep between ** once, rep between * across, turn. (142 [156, 170, 184, 198, 212] sc)

**SMALL, X-LARGE &
2X-LARGE SIZES ONLY**
Row 5: Ch 1, sc in back lp of first st, sc in front lp of next st, [sc in back lp of next sc, sc in front lp of next sc] across, turn.

**MEDIUM, LARGE &
3X-LARGE SIZES ONLY**
Row [5]: Ch 1, sc in back lp of first st, sc in front lp of next st, *[sc in back lp of next sc, sc in front lp of next sc]* [19, 21, 26] times, **[sc in back lp of next sc, sc in front lp of same sc] twice**, rep between * [38, 41, 52] times, rep between ** once, rep between * across, turn. ([160, 174, 216] sc)

RIGHT FRONT
SMALL, LARGE & 2X-LARGE SIZES ONLY
Row 1: Ch 1, sc in front lp of first st, sc in back lp of next st, [sc in front lp of next sc, sc in back lp of next sc] 17 [21, 24] times, leaving rem sts unworked, turn. (36 [44, 50] sc)

**MEDIUM, X-LARGE &
3X-LARGE SIZES ONLY**
Row [1]: Ch 1, sc in front lp of first st, sc in back lp of next st, [sc in front lp of next sc, sc in back lp of next sc] [19, 22, 26] times, leaving rem sts unworked, turn. ([40, 46, 54] sc)

ALL SIZES
Row 2: Ch 5, sc in 2nd ch from hook and in each of next 3 chs, [sc in back lp of next sc, sc in front lp of next sc] across, turn. (40 [44, 48, 50, 54, 58] sc)

Row 3: Ch 1, sc in front lp of first st, sc in back lp of next st, *sc in front lp of next sc**, sc in back lp of next sc, rep from * across, ending last rep at **, **ext sc** (*see Special Stitch*) in last sc, [ext sc in first step of last ext sc] 4 times, turn. (44 [48, 52, 54, 58, 62] sc)

Next rows: [Rep rows 2 and 3 alternately] 1 [5, 2, 5, 4, 4] time(s). (52 [88, 68, 94, 90, 94] sc)

UNDERARM SHAPING

Row 1: Ch 7 [7, 7, 3, 3, 3], sc in 2nd ch from hook and in each ch across, [sc in back lp of next sc, sc in front lp of next sc] across, turn. (58 [94, 74, 96, 92, 96] sc)

SMALL, LARGE, X-LARGE, 2X-LARGE & 3X-LARGE SIZES ONLY

Row 2: Ch 1, sc in front lp of first st, sc in back lp of next st, *sc in front lp of next sc**, sc in back lp of next sc, rep from * across, ending last rep at **, ext sc in last sc, [ext sc in first step of last sc] 6 [6, 2, 2, 2] times, turn. (64 [80, 98, 94, 98] sc)

Next rows: [Rep rows 1 and 2 alternately] 2 [1, 0, 1, 1] time(s). (88 [92, 98, 98, 102] sc)

Next row: Ch 5 [7, 3, 5, 3], sc in 2nd ch from hook and in each ch across, [sc in back lp of next sc, sc in front lp of next sc] across, turn. (92 [98, 100, 102, 104] sc)

SLEEVE
ALL SIZES

Row 1: Ch 1, sc in front lp of first st, sc in back lp of next st, [sc in front lp of next sc, sc in back lp of next sc] across, turn.

Row 2: Ch 1, sc in back lp of first st, sc in front lp of next st, [sc in back lp of next sc, sc in front lp of next sc] across, turn.

Next rows: [Rep rows 1 and 2 alternately] 3 [3, 5, 4, 5, 6] times.

Next row: Rep row 1.

SHOULDER SHAPING

Row 1: Ch 1, sc in back lp of first st, sc in front lp of next st, [sc in back lp of next sc, sc in front lp of next sc] across, leaving last 10 [10, 12, 12, 14, 14] sts unworked, turn. (82 [84, 86, 88, 88, 90] sc)

Row 2: Ch 1, sc in front lp of first st, sc in back lp of next st, [sc in front lp of next sc, sc in back lp of next sc] across, turn.

Row 3: Ch 1, sc in back lp of first st, sc in front lp of next st, [sc in back lp of next sc, sc in front lp of next sc] across, turn.

Rows 4 & 5: Rep rows 2 and 3.

Row 6: Ch 1, sc in front lp of first st, sc in back lp of next st, [sc in front lp of next sc, sc in back lp of next sc] 7 [7, 7, 8, 8, 8] times, sl st in next sc, leaving rem sts unworked. Fasten off. *(16 [16, 16, 18, 18, 18] sc)*

LEFT FRONT
Row 1: With RS facing, sk next 70 [80, 86, 92, 98, 108] sc on Bodice, **join** *(see Pattern Notes)* in next sc, ch 1, sc in front lp of same sc, *sc in back lp of next sc**, sc in front lp of next sc, rep from * across, ending last rep at **, turn. *(36 [40, 44, 46, 50, 54] sc)*

Row 2: Ch 1, sc in back lp of first st, sc in front lp of next st, *sc in back lp of next sc**, sc in front lp of next sc, rep from * across, ending last rep at **, ext sc in last sc, [ext sc in first step of last ext sc] 4 times, turn. *(40 [44, 48, 50, 54, 58] sc)*

Row 3: Ch 5, sc in 2nd ch from hook and in each of next 3 chs, [sc in front lp of next sc, sc in back lp of next sc] across, turn. *(44 [48, 52, 54, 58, 62] sc)*

Next rows: [Rep rows 2 and 3 alternately] 1 [5, 2, 5, 4, 4] time(s). *(52 [88, 68, 94, 90, 94] sc)*

UNDERARM SHAPING
Row 1: Ch 1, sc in back lp of first st, sc in front lp of next st, *sc in back lp of next sc**, sc in front lp of next sc, rep from * across, ending last rep at **, ext sc in last sc, [ext sc in first step of last sc] 6 [6, 6, 2, 2, 2] times, turn. *(58 [94, 74, 96, 92, 96] sc)*

SMALL, LARGE, X-LARGE, 2X-LARGE & 3X-LARGE SIZES ONLY
Row 2: Ch 7 [7, 3, 3, 3], sc in 2nd ch from hook and in each ch across, [sc in front lp of next sc, sc in back lp of next sc] across, turn. *(64 [80, 98, 94, 98] sc)*

Next rows: [Rep rows 1 and 2 alternately] 2 [1, 0, 1, 1] time(s). *(88 [92, 98, 98, 102] sc)*

Next row: Ch 1, sc in back lp of first st, sc in front lp of next st, *sc in back lp of next sc**, sc in front lp of next sc, rep from * across,

ending last rep at **, ext sc in last sc, [ext sc in first step of last sc] 4 [6, 2, 4, 2] times, turn. *(92 [98, 100, 102, 104] sc)*

SLEEVE
ALL SIZES
Row 1: Ch 1, sc in front lp of first st, sc in back lp of next st, [sc in front lp of next sc, sc in back lp of next sc] across, turn.

Row 2: Ch 1, sc in back lp of first st, sc in front lp of next st, [sc in back lp of next sc, sc in front lp of next sc] across, turn.

Next rows: [Rep rows 1 and 2 alternately] 3 [3, 5, 4, 5, 6] times.

Next row: Rep row 1.

SHOULDER SHAPING
Row 1: Sl st in each of first 10 [10, 12, 12, 14, 14] sc, [sc in back lp of next sc, sc in front lp of next sc] across, turn. *(82 [84, 86, 88, 88, 90] sc)*

Row 2: Ch 1, sc in front lp of first st, sc in back lp of next st, [sc in front lp of next sc, sc in back lp of next sc] across, turn.

Row 3: Ch 1, sc in back lp of first st, sc in front lp of next st, [sc in back lp of next sc, sc in front lp of next sc] across, turn.

Rows 4 & 5: Rep rows 2 and 3. At end of last row, fasten off.

Row 6: With RS facing, sk next 65 [67, 69, 69, 69, 71] sc, join in next sc, ch 1, [sc in front lp of next sc, sc in back lp of next sc] across. Fasten off. *(16 [16, 16, 18, 18, 18] sc)*

BACK
SMALL, LARGE & 2X-LARGE SIZES ONLY
Row 1: With RS facing and working in last row of Bodice, join in first unworked sc, ch 1, sc in front lp of same sc, ◊*[sc in back lp of next sc*, sc in front lp of next sc] 16 [20, 23] times, rep between * once◊, [sc in front lp of next sc, sc in back lp of same sc] twice, sc in front lp of next sc, rep between ◊ once, turn. *(72 [88, 100] sc)*

MEDIUM, X-LARGE & 3X-LARGE SIZES ONLY
Row [1]: With RS facing and working in last row of Bodice, join in first unworked sc, ch 1, sc in front lp of same sc, *sc in back lp of next sc**, sc in front lp of next sc, rep from * across, ending last rep at **, turn. *([80, 92, 108] sc)*

ALL SIZES
Row 2: Ch 5, sc in 2nd ch from hook and in each of next 3 chs, *sc in back lp of next sc**, sc in front lp of next sc, rep from * across, ending last rep at **, ext sc in last sc, [ext sc in first step of last sc] 4 times, turn. *(80 [88, 96, 100, 108, 116] sc)*

Row 3: Ch 5, sc in 2nd ch from hook and in each of next 3 chs, *sc in front lp of next sc**, sc in back lp of next sc, rep from * across, ending last rep at **, ext sc in last sc, [ext sc in first step of last sc] 4 times, turn. *(88 [96, 104, 108, 116, 124] sc)*

Next rows: [Rep rows 2 and 3 alternately] 1 [5, 2, 5, 4, 4] time(s). *(104 [176, 136, 188, 180, 188] sc)*

UNDERARM SHAPING
Row 1: Ch 7 [7, 7, 3, 3, 3], sc in 2nd ch from hook and in each ch across, *sc in back lp of next sc**, sc in front lp of next sc, rep from * across, ending last rep at **, ext sc in last sc, [ext sc in first step of last sc] 6 [6, 6, 2, 2, 2] times, turn. *(116 [188, 148, 192, 184, 192] sc)*

SMALL, LARGE, X-LARGE, 2X-LARGE & 3X-LARGE SIZES ONLY
Row 2: Ch 7 [7, 3, 3, 3], sc in 2nd ch from hook and in each ch across, *sc in front lp of next sc**, sc in back lp of next sc, rep from * across, ending last rep at **, ext sc in last sc, [ext sc in 1st step of last sc] 6 [6, 2, 2, 2] times, turn. *(128 [160, 196, 188, 196] sc)*

Next rows: [Rep rows 1 and 2 alternately] 2 [1, 0, 1, 1] time(s). *(176 [184, 196, 196, 204] sc)*

Next row: Ch 5 [7, 3, 5, 3], sc in 2nd ch from hook and in each ch across, *sc in back lp of next sc, sc in front lp of next sc, rep from * across, ending last rep at **, ext sc in last sc, [ext sc in first step of last sc] 4 [6, 2, 4, 2] times, turn. *(184 [188, 196, 200, 204, 208] sc)*

SLEEVE
ALL SIZES
Row 1: Ch 1, sc in front lp of first st, sc in back lp of next st, [sc in front lp of next sc, sc in back lp of next sc] across, turn. *(184 [188, 196, 200, 204, 208] sc)*

Row 2: Ch 1, sc in back lp of first st, sc in front lp of next st, [sc in back lp of next sc, sc in front lp of next sc] across, turn.

Next rows: [Rep rows 1 and 2 alternately] 5 [5, 7, 6, 7, 8] times.

Next row: Rep row 1.

LEFT SHOULDER
Row 1: Ch 1, sc in back lp of first st, sc in front lp of next st, [sc in back lp of next sc, sc in front lp of next sc] 40 [41, 42, 43, 43, 44] times, leaving rem sts unworked, turn. *(82 [84, 86, 88, 88, 90] sc)*

Row 2: Holding Left Front and Back Sleeves RS tog, sl st in front lp of first sc of Front, sc in front lp of first sc of Back, *sl st in back lp of next sc of Front, sc in back lp of next sc of Back**, sl st in front lp of next sc of Front, sc in front lp of next sc of Back, rep from * across, ending last rep at **, sl st in last sc of Front. Fasten off.

RIGHT SHOULDER

Row 1: With WS facing, sk 20 [20, 24, 24, 28, 28] sc, join in next sc, ch 1, [sc in back lp of next sc, sc in front lp of next sc] across, turn. (82 [84, 86, 88, 88, 90] sc)

Row 2: Holding Right Front and Back Sleeves RS tog, sl st in front lp of first sc of Front, sc in front lp of first sc of Back, *sl st in back lp of next sc of Front, sc in back lp of next sc of Back**, sl st in front lp of next sc of Front, sc in front lp of next sc of Back, rep from * across, ending last rep at **, sl st in last sc of Front. Fasten off.

COLLAR BAND

Row 1: Now working in sts and ends of rows across neck edge, join in first sc on WS of Left Front, ch 1, sc in back lp of same sc, *[sc in front lp of next sc, sc in back lp of next sc] 4 [4, 5, 5, 6, 6] times*, **sc dec in next sc and next row, sc in each of next 6 rows, sc dec in next row and next sc**, sc in each of next 18 [18, 22, 22, 26, 26] sc, rep between ** once, rep between * once, sc in front lp of last sc, turn. (52 [52, 60, 60, 68, 68] sc)

Row 2: Ch 1, sc in front lp of first st, sc in back lp of next st, [sc in front lp of next sc, sc in back lp of next sc] across, turn.

Row 3: Ch 1, sc in back lp of first st, sc in front lp of next st, [sc in back lp of next sc, sc in front lp of next sc] across, turn.

COLLAR SHAPING
SMALL & MEDIUM SIZES ONLY
Row 1: Ch 1, sc in front lp of first st, sc in back lp of next st, **[sc in front lp of next sc, sc in back lp of next sc]** twice, ◊*[sc in front lp of next sc, sc in back lp of same sc] twice*, rep between ** 6 times, rep from ◊ twice, rep between * once, rep between ** twice, turn. (60 sc)

Row 2: Ch 1, sc in back lp of first st, sc in front lp of next st, [sc in back lp of next sc, sc in front lp of next sc] across, turn.

SMALL, MEDIUM, LARGE & X-LARGE SIZES ONLY
Row 3 [3, 1, 1]: Ch 1, sc in front lp of first st, sc in back lp of next st, [sc in front lp of next sc, sc in back lp of next sc] across, turn.

Row 4 [4, 2, 2]: Ch 1, sc in back lp of first sc, *[sc in front lp of next sc, sc in back lp of next sc]* twice, ◊**[sc in front lp of next sc, sc in back lp of same sc] twice**, rep between * 7 times, rep from ◊ twice, rep between ** once, rep between * twice, sc in front lp of last sc, turn. (68 sc)

COLLAR
ALL SIZES
Row 1: Ch 1, sc in front lp of first st, sc in back lp of next st, [sc in front lp of next sc, sc in back lp of next sc] across, turn.

Row 2: Ch 1, sc in back lp of first st, sc in front lp of next st, [sc in back lp of next sc, sc in front lp of next sc] across, turn.

Row 3: Ch 1, sc in front lp of first st, sc in back lp of next st, *[sc in front lp of next sc, sc in back lp of next sc]* twice, ◊**[sc in front lp of next sc, sc in back lp of same sc] twice**, rep between * 8 times, rep from ◊ twice, rep between ** once, rep between * 3 times, turn. (76 sc)

Row 4: Rep row 2.

Row 5: Rep row 1.

Row 6: Ch 1, sc in back lp of first sc, *[sc in front lp of next sc, sc in back lp of next sc]* 3 times, ◊**[sc in front lp of next sc, sc in back lp of same sc] twice**, rep between * 9 times, rep from ◊ twice, rep between ** once, rep between * 3 times, sc in front lp of last sc, turn. (84 sc)

Rows 7 & 8: Rep rows 1 and 2.

Row 9: Ch 1, sc in front lp of first st, sc in back lp of next st, *[sc in front lp of next sc, sc in back lp of next sc]* 3 times, ◊**[sc in front lp of next sc, sc in back lp of same sc] twice**, rep between * 10 times, rep from ◊ twice, rep between ** once, rep between * 4 times, turn. (92 sc)

Row 10: Rep row 2.

Row 11: Rep row 1.

LARGE, X-LARGE, 2X-LARGE & 3X-LARGE SIZES ONLY
Row [12]: Ch 1, sc in back lp of first sc, *[sc in front lp of next sc, sc in back lp of next sc]* 4 times, ◊**[sc in front lp of next sc, sc in back lp of same sc] twice**, rep between * 11 times, rep from ◊ twice, rep between ** once, rep between * 4 times, sc in front lp of last sc, turn. (100 sc)

Rows [13 & 14]: Rep rows 1 and 2.

Row [15]: Ch 1, sc in front lp of first st, sc in back lp of next st, *[sc in front lp of next sc, sc in back lp of next sc]* 4 times, ◊**[sc in front lp of next sc, sc in back lp of same sc] twice**, rep between * 12 times, rep from ◊ twice, rep between ** once, rep between * 5 times, turn. (108 sc)

Row 16: Rep row 2.

Row 17: Rep row 1.

LARGE & X-LARGE SIZES ONLY
Row [18]: Rep row 2.

2X-LARGE & 3X-LARGE SIZES ONLY
Row [18]: Ch 1, sc in back lp of first sc, *[sc in front lp of next sc, sc in back lp of next sc]* 5 times, ◊**[sc in front lp of next sc, sc in back lp of same sc] twice**, rep between * 13 times, rep from ◊ twice, rep between ** once, rep between * 5 times, sc in front lp of last sc, turn. (116 sc)

Rows [19 & 20]: Rep rows 1 and 2.

Row [21]: Ch 1, sc in front lp of first st, sc in back lp of next st, *[sc in front lp of next sc, sc in back lp of next sc]* 5 times, ◊**[sc in front lp of next sc, sc in back lp of same sc] twice**, rep between * 14 times, rep from ◊ twice, rep between ** once, rep between * 6 times, turn. *(124 sc)*

Row [22]: Rep row 2.

Row [23]: Rep row 1. At end of row, **do not turn.**

BUTTON BAND
LEFT FRONT
Row 1: Working along front edge, evenly sp 121 [125, 131, 135, 139, 143] sc across, turn. *(121 [125, 131, 135, 139, 143] sc)*

Row 2: Ch 1, sc in front lp of each sc across, turn.

Row 3: Ch 1, sc in each sc across, turn.

Row 4: Rep row 2. Fasten off.

RIGHT FRONT
Row 1: With RS facing, working in sts and ends of rows, join in first sc, ch 1, sc in same st, evenly sp, 120 [124, 130, 134, 138, 142] sc across, turn. *(121 [125, 131, 135, 139, 143] sc)*

Row 2: Ch 1, sc in each of first 21 [21, 25, 25, 29, 29] sc, ch 2, sk next 2 sc, *sc in each of next 11 [12, 12, 13, 13, 14] sc, ch 2, sk next 2 sc, rep from * 4 times, sc in each rem sc across, turn. *(109 [113, 119, 123, 127, 131] sc, 6 ch-2 sps)*

Row 3: Ch 1, sc in each sc, 2 sc in each ch-2 sp across, turn. *(121 [125, 131, 135, 139, 143] sc)*

Row 4: Ch 1, sc in each sc across, turn.

TRIM
With RS facing, working in ends of rows and in sts, *sc in back lp of each of next 100 [104, 106, 110, 110, 114] sc*, sc in front lp of each sc around Collar, with 3 sc in each corner, rep between * once, sc in end of each row along bottom edge, join in beg sc. Fasten off.

FINISHING

Sew Sleeves tog at underarms. On RS of Sleeve opening at seam, join, ch 1, working in ends of rows, sc in each row around, join in beg sc. Fasten off.

Sew buttons to Left Front Button Band opposite buttonholes on Right Front Band. ■

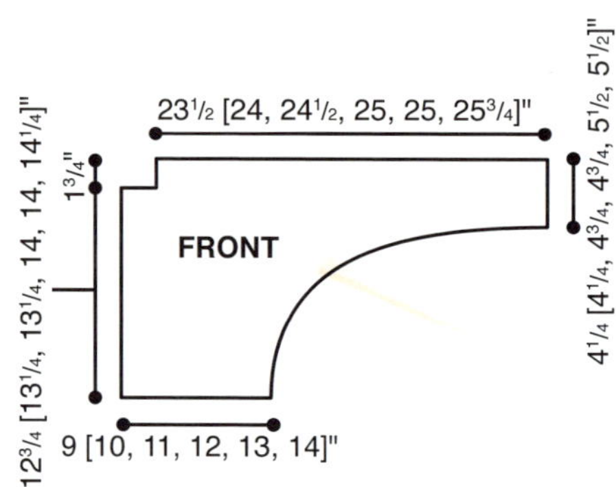

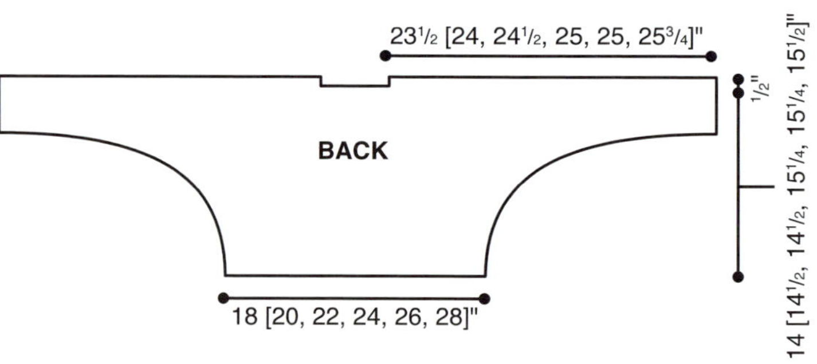

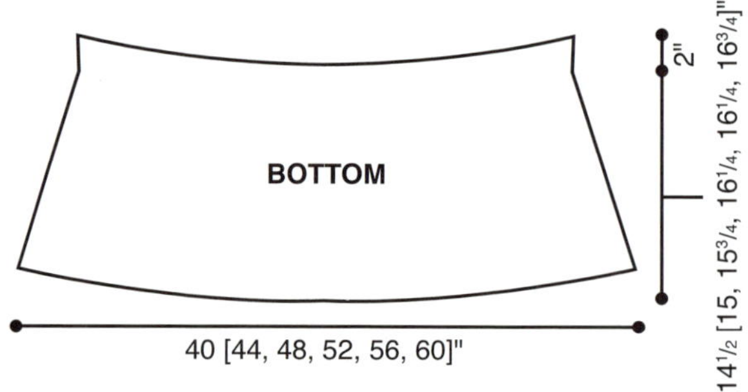

STITCH GUIDE

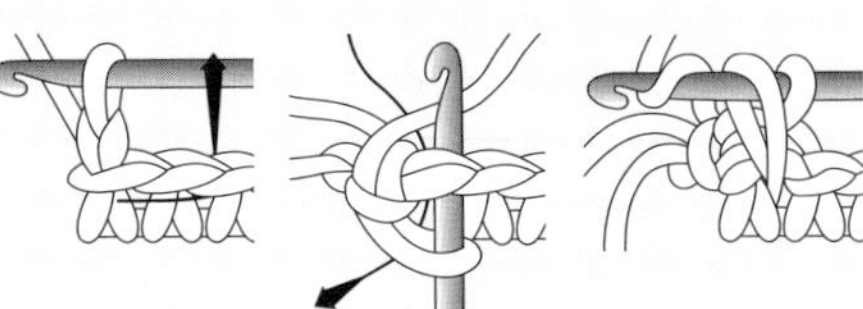

STITCH ABBREVIATIONS

beg	begin/begins/beginning
bpdc	back post double crochet
bpsc	back post single crochet
bptr	back post treble crochet
CC	contrasting color
ch(s)	chain(s)
ch-	refers to chain or space previously made (i.e., ch-1 space)
ch sp(s)	chain space(s)
cl(s)	cluster(s)
cm	centimeter(s)
dc	double crochet (singular/plural)
dc dec	double crochet 2 or more stitches together, as indicated
dec	decrease/decreases/decreasing
dtr	double treble crochet
ext	extended
fpdc	front post double crochet
fpsc	front post single crochet
fptr	front post treble crochet
g	gram(s)
hdc	half double crochet
hdc dec	half double crochet 2 or more stitches together, as indicated
inc	increase/increases/increasing
lp(s)	loop(s)
MC	main color
mm	millimeter(s)
oz	ounce(s)
pc	popcorn(s)
rem	remain/remains/remaining
rep(s)	repeat(s)
rnd(s)	round(s)
RS	right side
sc	single crochet (singular/plural)
sc dec	single crochet 2 or more stitches together, as indicated
sk	skip/skipped/skipping
sl st(s)	slip stitch(es)
sp(s)	space(s)/spaced
st(s)	stitch(es)
tog	together
tr	treble crochet
trtr	triple treble
WS	wrong side
yd(s)	yard(s)
yo	yarn over

YARN CONVERSION

OUNCES TO GRAMS		GRAMS TO OUNCES	
1	28.4	25	7/8
2	56.7	40	1 2/3
3	85.0	50	1 3/4
4	113.4	100	3 1/2

UNITED STATES		UNITED KINGDOM
sl st (slip stitch)	=	sc (single crochet)
sc (single crochet)	=	dc (double crochet)
hdc (half double crochet)	=	htr (half treble crochet)
dc (double crochet)	=	tr (treble crochet)
tr (treble crochet)	=	dtr (double treble crochet)
dtr (double treble crochet)	=	ttr (triple treble crochet)
skip	=	miss

Reverse Single Crochet (reverse sc): Ch 1. Skip first st. [Working from left to right, insert hook in next st from front to back, draw up lp on hook, yo, and draw through both lps on hook.]

Chain (ch): Yo, pull through lp on hook.

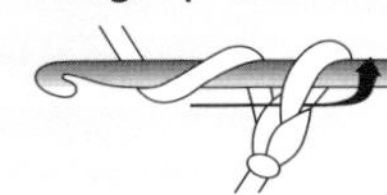

Single crochet (sc): Insert hook in st, yo, pull through st, yo, pull through both lps on hook.

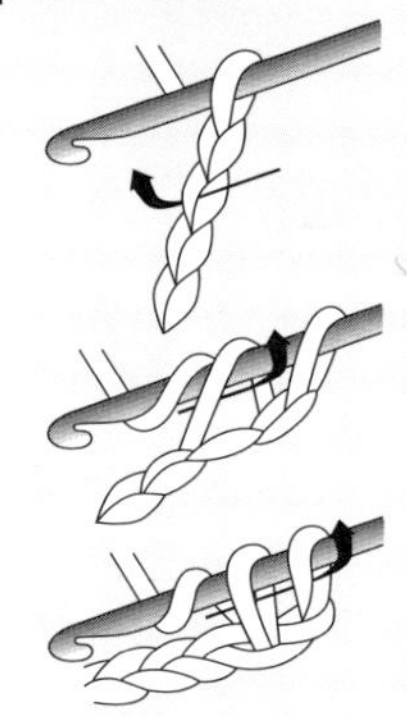

Double crochet (dc): Yo, insert hook in st, yo, pull through st, [yo, pull through 2 lps] twice.

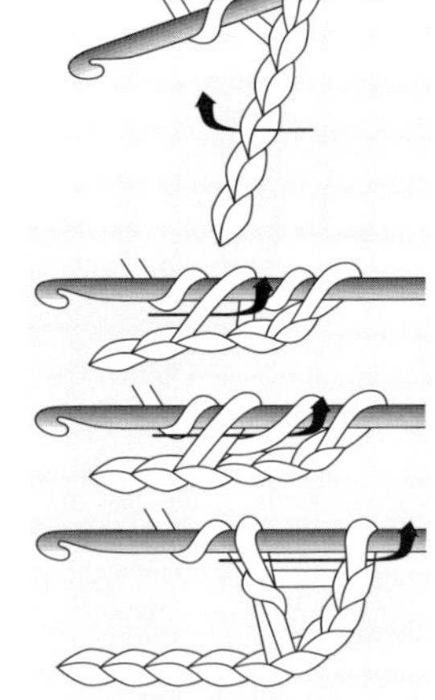

Front loop (front lp) Back loop (back lp)

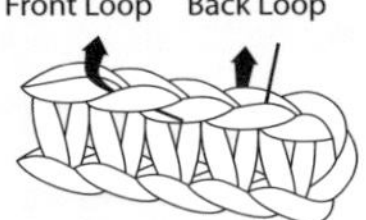

Front post stitch (fp): Back post stitch (bp): When working post st, insert hook from right to left around post st on previous row.

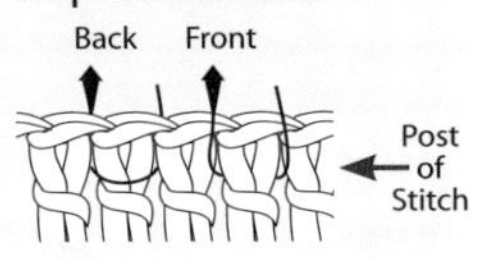

Half double crochet (hdc): Yo, insert hook in st, yo, pull through st, yo, pull through all 3 lps on hook.

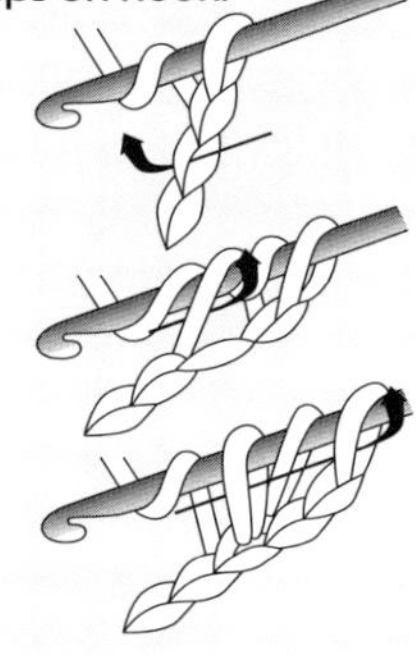

Double treble crochet (dtr): Yo 3 times, insert hook in st, yo, pull through st, [yo, pull through 2 lps] 4 times.

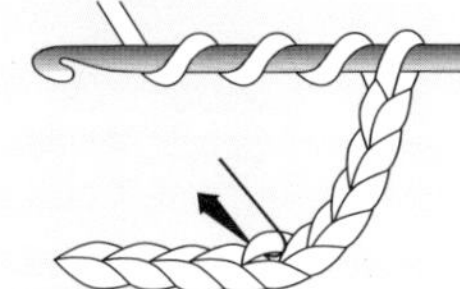

Slip stitch (sl st): Insert hook in st, pull through both lps on hook.

Chain Color Change (ch color change) Yo with new color, draw through last lp on hook.

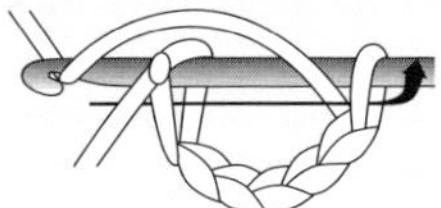

Double Crochet Color Change (dc color change) Drop first color, yo with new color, draw through last 2 lps of st.

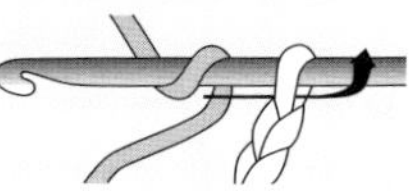

Treble crochet (tr): Yo twice, insert hook in st, yo, pull through st, [yo, pull through 2 lps] 3 times.

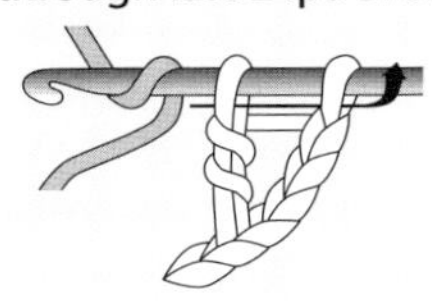

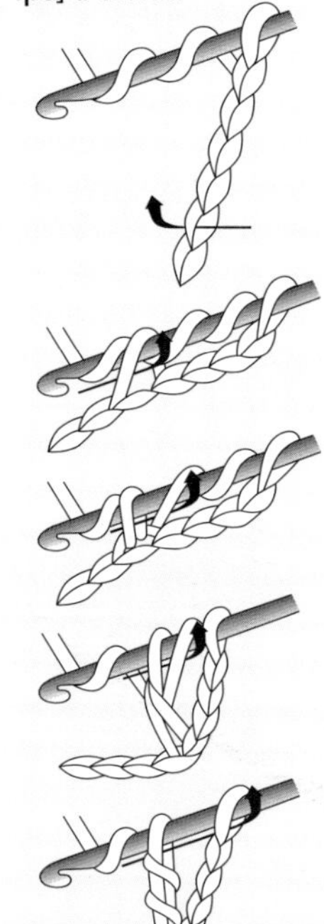

Single crochet decrease (sc dec): (Insert hook, yo, draw lp through) in each of the sts indicated, yo, draw through all lps on hook.

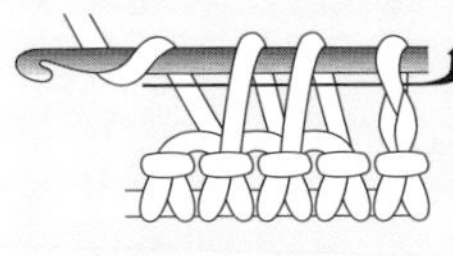

Example of 2-sc dec

Half double crochet decrease (hdc dec): (Yo, insert hook, yo, draw lp through) in each of the sts indicated, yo, draw through all lps on hook.

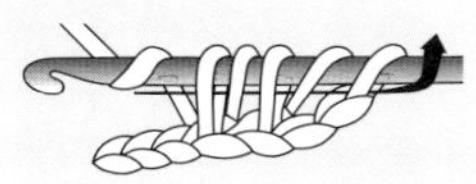

Example of 2-hdc dec

Double crochet decrease (dc dec): Yo, insert hook, yo, draw loop through, draw through 2 lps on hook) in each of the sts indicated, yo, draw through all lps on hook.

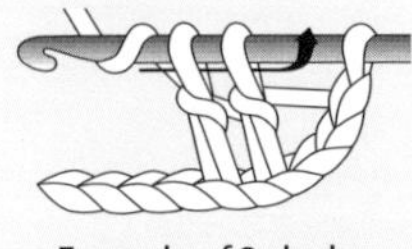

Example of 2-dc dec

Treble crochet decrease (tr dec): Holding back last lp of each st, tr in each of the sts indicated, yo, pull through all lps on hook.

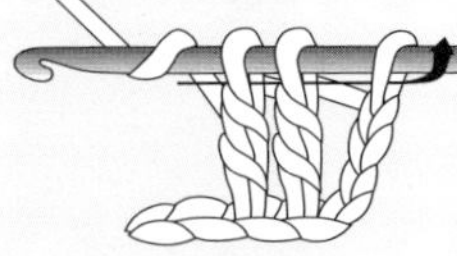

Example of 2-tr dec

Metric Conversion Charts

METRIC CONVERSIONS

yards	x	.9144	=	metres (m)
yards	x	91.44	=	centimetres (cm)
inches	x	2.54	=	centimetres (cm)
inches	x	25.40	=	millimetres (mm)
inches	x	.0254	=	metres (m)

centimetres	x	.3937	=	inches
metres	x	1.0936	=	yards

INCHES INTO MILLIMETRES & CENTIMETRES (Rounded off slightly)

inches	mm	cm	inches	cm	inches	cm	inches	cm
1/8	3	0.3	5	12.5	21	53.5	38	96.5
1/4	6	0.6	5 1/2	14	22	56	39	99
3/8	10	1	6	15	23	58.5	40	101.5
1/2	13	1.3	7	18	24	61	41	104
5/8	15	1.5	8	20.5	25	63.5	42	106.5
3/4	20	2	9	23	26	66	43	109
7/8	22	2.2	10	25.5	27	68.5	44	112
1	25	2.5	11	28	28	71	45	114.5
1 1/4	32	3.2	12	30.5	29	73.5	46	117
1 1/2	38	3.8	13	33	30	76	47	119.5
1 3/4	45	4.5	14	35.5	31	79	48	122
2	50	5	15	38	32	81.5	49	124.5
2 1/2	65	6.5	16	40.5	33	84	50	127
3	75	7.5	17	43	34	86.5		
3 1/2	90	9	18	46	35	89		
4	100	10	19	48.5	36	91.5		
4 1/2	115	11.5	20	51	37	94		

KNITTING NEEDLES CONVERSION CHART

Canada/U.S.	0	1	2	3	4	5	6	7	8	9	10	10½	11	13	15
Metric (mm)	2	2¼	2¾	3¼	3½	3¾	4	4½	5	5½	6	6½	8	9	10

CROCHET HOOKS CONVERSION CHART

Canada/U.S.	1/B	2/C	3/D	4/E	5/F	6/G	8/H	9/I	10/J	10½/K	N
Metric (mm)	2.25	2.75	3.25	3.5	3.75	4.25	5	5.5	6	6.5	9.0